Taste of Home

prize
winning
recipes

Reader's Digest

The Reader's Digest Association, Inc.
Pleasantville, NY/Montreal

Reader's Digest and Taste of Home are registered trademarks of The Reader's Digest Association, Inc.

Pictured on Front Cover: Pear Custard Bars, page 115; Pork and Pear Stir-Fry, page 116.

Pictured on Back Cover: Breakfast Pockets, page 11; Chunky Beef Noodle Soup, page 84; Custard Bars, page 115.

For more Reader's Digest products and information, visit our website at www.rd.com

Printed in China

Editor: Jean Steiner
Art Director: Nicholas Mork
Executive Editor: Heidi Reuter Lloyd
Associate Editor: Beth Wittlinger
Graphic Art Associates: Ellen Lloyd, Catherine Fletcher
Food Editor: Janaan Cunningham
Associate Food Editors: Coleen Martin, Diane Werner
Senior Recipe Editor: Sue A. Jurack
Recipe Editor: Janet Briggs
Food Photography: Rob Hagen, Dan Roberts
Set Sylists: Julie Ferron, Sue Myers
Associate Set Stylist: Jennifer Bradley Vent
Senior Vice President, Editor in Chief: Catherine Cassidy
President: Barbara Newton
Chairman and Founder: Roy Reiman

contents

prize-winning recipes

Who decides that a recipe is prize-winning? Can I get my family's favorite ground beef dish published? These are just some of the questions you may have as you open this compilation of recipes from the readers of *Taste of Home*, America's most popular cooking magazine with nearly 4 million subscribers, or its "sister" publications, *Country Woman* and *Quick Cooking*. Included in every issue is a national contest, inviting readers to send in their very best recipes. After much sorting through piles of mail, testing in professional kitchens, and tasting by a panel of judges, a Grand Prize Winner and 11 runners-up are selected. The 180 recipes that make up this collection represent some of the winning favorites from 15 of these national contests.

The recipes are organized for easy use, including such favorite categories as Meat-and-Potato Combos, Comforting Casseroles, Sensational Soups, Super Salads, and more. Each of the 15 sections begins with a full-page, full-color photograph next to the Grand Prize Winner, with a few words about the dish from the winner. The runner-up recipes are also accompanied by a smaller eye-catching photo, and as a special treat, under the title of each recipe is a lively anecdote from the contributor as well. In a very personal way, each note makes the recipe itself more inviting. Wouldn't you love to make something that reminds you of your mother or grandmother, that gets you compliments, or makes it easier to make your favorite dessert? Here's what a few of our great cooks have to say about their special dishes:

> I give all the credit for my love of cooking and baking to my mother, grandmother, and mother-in-law. That trio inspired delicious dishes like this hearty skillet dinner. When we get a taste for stir-fry, this dish hits the spot.
>
> *Helen Carpenter, Marble Falls, Texas—Pork Chow Mein*

When I came up with this recipe, I was looking for something that didn't require last-minute fuss. It's great getting compliments on something so simple.
Myrtle Nelson, Wetaskinwin, Alberta—Chicken Potato Bake

It never occurred to me that I could bake a cobbler in my slow cooker until I saw some recipes and decided to try my favorite fruity dessert recipe. It took a bit of experimenting, but the results are 'berry' well worth it.
Martha Creveling, Orlando, Florida—Black and Blue Cobbler

Sprinkled throughout the recipes are practical prize-winning tips that even seasoned cooks will love. Did you know that you can save both time and money by buying ground beef in large quantity and cooking it, then freezing it in serving-size portions? That you can make a pork roast even tastier by topping it with a jar of all-fruit apricot preserves? That you can ripen pears at room temperature by placing them in a paper bag with an apple? That instead of boiling eggs for egg salad, you can poach them until the yolks are cooked through and you've saved time and don't even have to peel them? There is so much more to cooking than reading a recipe, and these helpful tips help you pick your ingredients, budget your time, and create a mouthwatering dish at the same time.

Finally, there is an easy-to-use index to help you select a dish by category that conforms to your occasion, your pantry, and your lifestyle. Whether you are looking for some party appetizers, a hearty casserole, or something to put on the grill, you will find a tempting array of possibilities at your fingertips.

All these recipes have been gathered from families across America and Canada and reflect the best-loved treasures of generations. Often the time-honored dish that has been passed down through the generations is adapted and becomes an extra special newfound dish that is added to the family treasure trove. Whether the dish is made on the stovetop, in the oven, in a slow cooker, or on the barbecue grill; whether it is meat, chicken, fish, or vegetable; whether it is simple or fancy, for weekday dining or a company feast—these delicious, home-tested recipes are sure to bring smiles to every family table and create memories to be savored for years to come.

PARTY APPETIZERS

#1

RYE PARTY PUFFS

Half the fun of a party or casual gathering is the lip-smacking lineup of finger foods. These tasty tidbits can be an appetizing prelude to—or even a substitute for—a meal.

A nice-to-nibble combination of spreads, dips, delicate baked bites, hearty stuffed morsels and more make up the winning recipes from our Party Appetizers contest. The 12 tempting tray-toppers here were selected from more than 4,000 entries.

"I can't go anywhere without taking along my puffs."

Any of these super snacks will make get-togethers truly tasteful affairs, especially Rye Party Puffs, which were chosen as the Grand Prize Winner.

"I can't go anywhere without taking along my puffs," says Kelly Thornberry of La Porte, Indiana. "They're pretty enough for a wedding reception yet also hearty enough to snack on while watching football on television. A platterful of these will disappear even with a small group."

        1 cup water
      1/2 cup butter
      1/2 cup all-purpose flour
      1/2 cup rye flour
        2 teaspoons dried parsley flakes
      1/2 teaspoon garlic powder
      1/4 teaspoon salt
        4 eggs
Caraway seeds
CORNED BEEF FILLING:
        2 packages (8 ounces *each*) cream cheese,
            softened
        2 packages (2-1/2 ounces *each*) thinly sliced
            cooked corned beef, chopped
      1/2 cup mayonnaise
      1/4 cup sour cream
        2 tablespoons minced chives
        2 tablespoons diced onion
        1 teaspoon spicy brown *or* horseradish mustard
      1/8 teaspoon garlic powder
       10 small stuffed olives, chopped

In a saucepan over medium heat, bring water and butter to a boil. Add flours, parsley, garlic powder and salt all at once; stir until a smooth ball forms. Remove from the heat; let stand for 5 minutes. Beat in eggs, one at time. Beat until smooth.

Drop batter by rounded teaspoonfuls 2 in. apart onto greased baking sheets. Sprinkle with caraway. Bake at 400° for 18-20 minutes or until golden. Remove to wire racks. Immediately cut a slit in each puff to allow steam to escape; cool.

In a mixing bowl, combine the first eight filling ingredients; mix well. Stir in olives. Split puffs; add filling. Refrigerate. **Yield:** 4-1/2 dozen.

savory bread strips

Mary Nichols, Dover, New Hampshire
The savory ingredients in this irresistible appetizer blend so well that I'm always asked for the recipe.

   1 package (1/4 ounce) active dry yeast
6-1/2 teaspoons sugar, *divided*
  1/2 cup warm water (110° to 115°)
   3 tablespoons olive oil
   2 tablespoons dried minced onion
   2 teaspoons dried basil
   1 teaspoon dried oregano
   1 teaspoon rubbed sage
   1 teaspoon garlic powder
  1/2 cup cold water
   3 cups all-purpose flour
TOPPING:
1-1/2 cups chopped fully cooked ham
   1 cup shredded Parmesan cheese
  1/2 cup chopped ripe olives
  1/2 cup chopped onion
  1/2 cup minced fresh parsley
  1/4 cup olive oil
   2 garlic cloves, minced

Dissolve yeast and 1/2 teaspoon sugar in warm water; set aside. In a saucepan, combine oil, onion, basil, oregano, sage and garlic powder; cook over medium heat for 1 minute. Remove from the heat; stir in cold water. In a mixing bowl, combine flour and remaining sugar. Stir in oil and yeast mixtures.

Turn onto a lightly floured surface; knead for 3 minutes. Place dough on a greased 15-in. x 10-in. x 1-in. baking pan. Cover and let stand for 15 minutes. Pat dough evenly into pan. Combine topping ingredients; sprinkle over dough. Bake at 375° for 25-30 minutes or until well browned. Cut into strips. **Yield:** about 6 dozen.

four-cheese pate

Jeanne Messina, Darien, Connecticut
This impressive and festive-looking cheese spread is simple to put together and never fails to get raves at parties.

   3 packages (8 ounces *each*) cream cheese, softened, *divided*
   2 tablespoons milk
   2 tablespoons sour cream
  3/4 cup chopped pecans
   4 ounces Brie *or* Camembert, rind removed, softened
   1 cup (4 ounces) shredded Swiss cheese
   4 ounces crumbled blue cheese
  1/2 cup pecan halves
Red and green apple slices *or* crackers

In a mixing bowl, beat one package of cream cheese with milk and sour cream until smooth. Spread into a 9-in. pie plate lined with plastic wrap. Sprinkle with chopped pecans.

In a mixing bowl, beat Brie, Swiss, blue cheese and remaining cream cheese until thoroughly combined. Gently spread over chopped pecans, smoothing the top to form a flat surface. Cover and chill overnight or up to 3-4 days.

Before serving, invert onto a plate and remove plastic wrap. Arrange pecan halves on top. Serve with apples or crackers. **Yield:** 16-20 servings.

appetizer roll-ups

Marcella Funk, Salem, Oregon

Cream cheese and a variety of herbs and vegetables make even deli cold cuts a fancy and filling appetizer. Bite-size pieces look so pretty set on a platter in a circle. But the arrangement never stays complete for very long once this snack is served.

ROAST BEEF:
    4 ounces cream cheese, softened
    1/4 cup minced fresh cilantro
    2 to 3 tablespoons minced banana peppers
    1 garlic clove, minced
    1/2 pound thinly sliced cooked roast beef
HAM AND TURKEY:
    12 ounces cream cheese, softened
    1/2 cup shredded carrot
    1/2 cup shredded zucchini
    4 teaspoons dill weed
    1/2 pound thinly sliced fully cooked ham
    1/2 pound thinly sliced cooked turkey

In a bowl, combine the cream cheese, cilantro, peppers and garlic. Spread about 2 tablespoons on each slice of beef. Roll up tightly and wrap in plastic wrap.

In another bowl, combine cream cheese, carrot, zucchini and dill. Spread about 2 tablespoons on each slice of ham and turkey. Roll up tightly; wrap in plastic wrap. Refrigerate overnight. Slice into 1-1/2-in. pieces. **Yield:** 6-7 dozen.

festive sausage cups

Gail Watkins, South Bend, Indiana

When I use prepared pie crust for this recipe, it's even easier to form and fill these individual sausage cups. They are a savory and filling snack. Come Thanksgiving and Christmas, my family is especially delighted to see them.

Pastry for double-crust pie (9 inches)
    1 pound bulk hot pork sausage
    6 green onions, chopped
    1 tablespoon butter
    1/2 cup chopped canned mushrooms
    1/4 cup thinly sliced stuffed olives
    3/4 teaspoon salt
    1/4 teaspoon pepper
    1/4 cup all-purpose flour
    2 cups heavy whipping cream
    1 cup (4 ounces) shredded Swiss cheese
Chopped stuffed olives

On a lightly floured surface, roll pastry to 1/8-in. thickness. Cut with a 2-1/2-in. round cookie cutter. Press onto the bottom and up the sides of greased miniature muffin cups. Bake at 400° for 6-8 minutes or until lightly browned. Remove from pans to cool on wire racks.

In a skillet, cook sausage over medium heat until no longer pink; drain and set aside. In the same skillet, saute onions in butter until tender. Add mushrooms, olives, salt and pepper. Sprinkle with flour. Add cream; bring to a boil, stirring constantly. Stir in sausage. Reduce heat; simmer until thickened, about 5-10 minutes, stirring constantly.

Spoon into pastry cups; sprinkle with cheese. Place on ungreased baking sheets. Bake at 350° for 10 minutes or until cheese is melted. Garnish with chopped olives. Serve hot. **Yield:** 4 dozen.

spiced nut mix

Patti Holland, Parker, Colorado

When we were newlyweds, our first Christmas was pretty lean. I usually make presents, but that year I had no idea what I could afford to put together. A good friend gave me a special gift—this recipe and a sack of ingredients. I think of her every time I stir up this mix.

> 3 egg whites
> 2 teaspoons water
> 2 cans (12 ounces *each*) salted peanuts
> 1 cup whole blanched almonds
> 1 cup walnut halves
> 1-3/4 cups sugar
> 3 tablespoons pumpkin pie spice
> 3/4 teaspoon salt
> 1 cup raisins

In a mixing bowl, beat egg whites and water until frothy. Add nuts; stir gently to coat. Combine sugar, pie spice and salt; add to nut mixture and stir gently to coat. Fold in raisins.

Spread into two greased 15-in. x 10-in. x 1-in. baking pans. Bake, uncovered, at 300° for 20-25 minutes or until lightly browned, stirring every 10 minutes. Cool completely. Store in an airtight container. **Yield:** about 10 cups.

tomato cheese pinwheels

Maggie Gassett, Hillsborough, New Hampshire

No matter how many of these pinwheels we bake, there are never any leftovers. The light cheddar tang complements the tomato flavor beautifully. They look complicated but are surprisingly easy to prepare.

> 4 to 4-1/2 cups all-purpose flour
> 2 tablespoons sugar
> 1 package (1/4 ounce) active dry yeast
> 1-1/4 teaspoons salt
> 3/4 cup warm tomato juice (120° to 130°)
> 1/2 cup warm water (120° to 130°)
> 1/4 cup butter
> 1 egg
> 2 cups (8 ounces) finely shredded sharp cheddar cheese
> 2 tablespoons snipped chives

In a mixing bowl, combine 1 cup flour, sugar, yeast and salt. Add tomato juice, water and butter; beat for 2 minutes on medium speed. Add egg and enough remaining flour to form a soft dough. Place in a greased bowl; turn once to grease top. Cover and refrigerate for 2 hours or until doubled.

Punch dough down. Divide in half; roll each half into a 15-in. x 12-in. rectangle approximately 1/8 in. thick. Cut into 3-in. squares. Place 2 in. apart on greased baking sheets. Make 1-in. slits in each corner of each square.

Combine cheese and chives; place 1 heaping teaspoon in the center of each square. Bring every other corner up to center, overlapping slightly to form a pinwheel; press firmly. Bake at 400° for 8-10 minutes. Remove to a wire rack to cool. **Yield:** 40 appetizers.

spinach turnovers

Jean von Bereghy, Oconomowoc, Wisconsin

The flaky cream cheese pastry adds sensational texture to these hot appetizers—and just wait until you taste the wonderful filling. I usually fix a double batch and freeze some to have on hand in case unexpected guests drop by.

- 2 packages (8 ounces *each*) cream cheese, softened
- 3/4 cup butter, softened
- 2-1/2 cups all-purpose flour
- 1/2 teaspoon salt

FILLING:

- 5 bacon strips, diced
- 1/4 cup finely chopped onion
- 2 garlic cloves, minced
- 1 package (10 ounces) frozen chopped spinach, thawed and well drained
- 1 cup small-curd cottage cheese
- 1/4 teaspoon salt
- 1/4 teaspoon pepper
- 1/8 teaspoon ground nutmeg
- 1 egg, beaten

Salsa, optional

In a mixing bowl, beat cream cheese and butter until smooth. Combine flour and salt; gradually add to creamed mixture (dough will be stiff). Turn onto a floured surface; gently knead 10 times. Cover and refrigerate at least 2 hours.

In a skillet, cook bacon until crisp. Remove bacon; reserve 1 tablespoon drippings. Saute onion and garlic in drippings until tender. Remove from heat; stir in bacon, spinach, cottage cheese and seasonings. Cool.

On a lightly floured surface, roll dough to 1/8-in. thickness. Cut into 3-in. circles; brush edges with egg. Place 1 heaping teaspoon of filling on each circle. Fold over; seal edges. Prick tops with a fork. Brush with egg. Bake at 400° for 10-12 minutes or until golden brown. Serve with salsa if desired. **Yield:** about 4 dozen.

Editor's Note: Baked turnovers may be frozen. Reheat unthawed turnovers at 400° for 10 minutes.

prize winningtips

* For a no-fuss appetizer, wrap 1 pound of bacon around 2 pounds of cocktail wieners. Use a toothpick to secure each bacon slice to a wiener. Place in a slow cooker and top with 1 pound of brown sugar. Heat on low 6 to 8 hours.

Deborah Loney, Central City, Kentucky

* I place dips in colorful edible bowls such as red or green cabbage shells, or cored sweet red, yellow or green peppers. Fruit dips can be spooned into melon, orange or grapefruit shells.

Janet Hamm, West Allis, Wisconsin

* Deviled eggs will be more stable, and sit flat without wobbling, if you cut off a tiny piece from the bottom of each half.

Diana Leskauskas, Chatham, New Jersey

hot macadamia spread

Naomi Francis, Waukesha, Wisconsin
While my husband was in the Army, I'd get together with other wives for snacks and an exchange of favorite recipes. I still enjoy serving this rich spread because most guests can't quite put their finger on the zippy ingredient—horseradish.

> 1 package (8 ounces) cream cheese, softened
> 2 tablespoons milk
> 1/2 cup sour cream
> 2 teaspoons prepared horseradish
> 1/4 cup finely chopped green pepper
> 1 green onion, chopped
> 1/2 teaspoon garlic salt
> 1/4 teaspoon pepper
> 1/2 cup chopped macadamia nuts *or* blanched almonds
> 2 teaspoons butter

Assorted crackers

In a mixing bowl, beat the cream cheese and milk until smooth. Stir in the sour cream, horseradish, green pepper, onion, garlic salt and pepper. Spoon the mixture into an ungreased shallow 2-cup baking dish and set aside.

In a skillet, saute the nuts in butter for 3-4 minutes or until lightly browned. Sprinkle over the cream cheese mixture. Bake, uncovered, at 350° for 20 minutes. Serve with crackers. **Yield:** 6-8 servings.

apricot wraps

Jane Ashworth, Beavercreek, Ohio
I accumulated a large recipe collection from around the world while my husband served in the Air Force for 25 years. This mouth-watering appetizer is one of our favorites, and we enjoy sharing it with family and friends. All you need to make the pretty, rolled wraps are five simple ingredients, which I like to keep on hand.

> 1 package (14 ounces) dried apricots
> 1/2 cup whole almonds
> 1 pound sliced bacon
> 1/4 cup plum *or* apple jelly
> 2 tablespoons soy sauce

Fold each apricot around a whole almond. Cut the bacon strips into thirds; wrap a strip around each apricot and secure with a toothpick.

Place on two ungreased 15-in. x 10-in. x 1-in. baking pans. Bake, uncovered, at 375° for 25 minutes or until the bacon is crisp, turning once.

In a small saucepan, combine the jelly and soy sauce; cook and stir over low heat for 5 minutes or until warmed and smooth. Remove apricots to paper towels; drain. Serve with the sauce for dipping. **Yield:** about 4-1/2 dozen.

avocado salsa

Susan Vandermeer, Ogden, Utah

When I found this recipe, I was planning a party and thought it might be a fun, different salsa to set out with chips. It was an absolute success. People love the garlic, corn and avocado combination. Now I'm often asked to bring it along to all sorts of gatherings.

>   1 package (16 ounces) frozen corn,
>   thawed
>   2 cans (2-1/4 ounces *each*) sliced ripe olives,
>   drained
>   1 medium sweet red pepper, chopped
>   1 small onion, chopped
>   5 garlic cloves, minced
> 1/3 cup olive oil
> 1/4 cup lemon juice
>   3 tablespoons white wine vinegar
>   1 teaspoon dried oregano
> 1/2 teaspoon salt
> 1/2 teaspoon pepper
>   4 medium ripe avocados

Tortilla chips

In a large bowl, combine corn, olives, red pepper and onion. In a small bowl, combine garlic, oil, lemon juice, vinegar, oregano, salt and pepper; mix well. Pour over corn mixture and toss to coat. Cover and refrigerate overnight.

Just before serving, chop avocados and stir into salsa. Serve with tortilla chips. **Yield:** about 7 cups.

twice-baked new potatoes

Susan Herbert, Aurora, Illinois

I've used these rich potatoes as both an appetizer and side dish. Guests seem to enjoy the distinctive taste of Monterey Jack cheese and basil. These satisfying mouthfuls are perfect for a late-afternoon or evening get-together when something a little heartier is needed.

> 1-1/2 pounds small red potatoes
>   2 to 3 tablespoons vegetable oil
>   1 cup (4 ounces) shredded Monterey Jack
>   cheese
>   1/2 cup sour cream
>   1 package (3 ounces) cream cheese, softened
>   1/3 cup minced green onions
>   1 teaspoon dried basil
>   1 garlic clove, minced
>   1/2 teaspoon salt
>   1/4 to 1/2 teaspoon pepper
>   1/2 pound sliced bacon, cooked and crumbled

Pierce potatoes; rub skins with oil. Place in a baking pan. Bake, uncovered, at 400° for 50 minutes or until tender. Allow to cool to the touch.

In a mixing bowl, combine Monterey Jack, sour cream, cream cheese, onions, basil, garlic, salt and pepper. Cut potatoes in half; carefully scoop out pulp, leaving a thin shell. Add pulp to the cheese mixture and mash; stir in bacon. Stuff potato shells. Broil for 7-8 minutes or until heated through. **Yield:** about 2 dozen.

BREAKFAST
POCKETS

BREAKFAST AND BRUNCH RECIPES

#1

I t's called the most important meal of the day. Sadly, though, some folks find breakfast just plain boring. Who wouldn't be bored with a piece of toast or a bowl of cold cereal?

Breakfast boredom is no problem for the thousands of subscribers who entered our Breakfast and Brunch Recipes contest, however. Their hearty, eye-opening family favorites make the morning meal what it was meant to be— a flavorful foundation to the whole day's activities.

"...serve a complete breakfast inside a tidy pocket of dough."

The coffee and conversation flowed freely as our panel of judges sampled those welcome wake-up dishes. The only thing missing was a morning paper! Breakfast Pockets, from Dolores Jantzen of Plymouth, Nebraska, were picked as the Grand Prize Winner.

"They may look somewhat plain on the outside, but the cheesy, meaty filling is far from ho-hum," says Dolores. "With these, I like being able to serve a complete breakfast inside a tidy pocket of dough."

    2 packages (1/4 ounce *each*) active dry yeast
1/2 cup warm water (110° to 115°)
3/4 cup warm evaporated milk (110° to 115°)
1/2 cup vegetable oil
1/4 cup sugar
    1 egg
    1 teaspoon salt
    3 to 4 cups all-purpose flour
FILLING:
    1 pound bulk pork sausage
1/2 cup chopped onion
2-1/2 cups frozen shredded hash browns, thawed
    7 eggs, lightly beaten
    3 tablespoons milk
1/2 teaspoon salt
1/2 teaspoon pepper
1/2 teaspoon garlic salt
Pinch cayenne pepper
    3 cups (12 ounces) shredded cheddar cheese

In a mixing bowl, dissolve yeast in water. Add evaporated milk, oil, sugar, egg, salt and 2 cups flour; beat until smooth. Add enough remaining flour to form a soft dough (do not knead). Cover and let rise in a warm place until doubled, about 1 hour.

Meanwhile, in a skillet, cook the sausage and onion over medium heat until sausage is no longer pink; drain. Add hash browns, eggs, milk and seasonings. Cook and stir until the eggs are completely set. Sprinkle with cheese; keep warm.

Punch dough down; divide into 14 pieces. On a floured surface, roll out dough into 7-in. circles. Top each with about 1/3 cup filling; fold dough over filling and pinch the edges to seal. Place on greased baking sheets. Bake at 350° for 15-20 minutes or until golden brown. **Yield:** 14 servings.

no-fry doughnuts

Susie Baldwin, Columbia, Tennessee
We have four boys, and these doughnuts never last long at our house. I like making them because I don't have to clean up a greasy mess.

- 2 packages (1/4 ounce *each*) active dry yeast
- 1/4 cup warm water (110° to 115°)
- 1-1/2 cups warm milk (110° to 115°)
- 1/3 cup shortening
- 1/2 cup sugar
- 2 eggs
- 1 teaspoon salt
- 1 teaspoon ground nutmeg
- 1/4 teaspoon ground cinnamon
- 4-1/2 to 5 cups all-purpose flour
- 1/4 cup butter, melted

GLAZE:
- 1/2 cup butter
- 2 cups confectioners' sugar
- 5 teaspoons water
- 2 teaspoons vanilla extract

In a mixing bowl, dissolve yeast in water. Add milk and shortening; stir for 1 minute. Add sugar, eggs, salt, nutmeg, cinnamon and 2 cups flour; beat on low speed until smooth. Stir in enough remaining flour to form a soft dough (do not knead). Cover and let rise in a warm place until doubled, about 1 hour.

Punch dough down. Turn onto a floured surface; roll out to 1/2-in. thickness. Cut with a 2-3/4-in. doughnut cutter; place 2 in. apart on greased baking sheets. Brush with butter. Cover and let rise in a warm place until doubled, about 30 minutes. Bake at 350° for 20 minutes or until lightly browned.

Meanwhile, in a saucepan, melt butter; stir in sugar, water and vanilla. Stir over low heat until smooth (do not boil). Keep warm. Dip warm doughnuts, one at a time, into glaze and turn to coat. Drain on a wire rack. Serve immediately. **Yield:** 2 dozen.

farmer's casserole

Nancy Schmidt, Center, Colorado
This casserole is handy—you can put it together the night before, let the flavors blend, then bake it in the morning. It's also versatile…elegant enough to serve for a ladies' brunch but hearty enough to satisfy a man-sized appetite.

- 3 cups frozen shredded hash browns
- 3/4 cup shredded Monterey Jack cheese
- 1 cup diced fully cooked ham
- 1/4 cup chopped green onions
- 4 eggs
- 1 can (12 ounces) evaporated milk
- 1/4 teaspoon pepper
- 1/8 teaspoon salt

Place potatoes in an 8-in. square baking dish. Sprinkle with cheese, ham and onions. Beat eggs, milk, pepper and salt; pour over all. Cover and refrigerate for several hours or overnight.

Remove from refrigerator 30 minutes before baking. Bake, uncovered, at 350° for 55-60 minutes or until a knife inserted near the center comes out clean. **Yield:** 6 servings.

make-ahead scrambled eggs

Diane Sackfield, Kingston, Ontario

I appreciate the convenience of this dish. I've served it for breakfast and also as part of a full brunch buffet along with breads, biscuits, bagels and side salads.

   5 tablespoons butter, *divided*
1/4 cup all-purpose flour
   2 cups milk
   2 cups (8 ounces) shredded cheddar cheese
   1 cup sliced fresh mushrooms
1/4 cup finely chopped onion
  12 eggs, beaten
   1 teaspoon salt
   1 package (10 ounces) frozen chopped broccoli, cooked and drained
   1 cup soft bread crumbs

In a saucepan, melt 2 tablespoons butter. Add flour; cook and stir until the mixture begins to bubble. Gradually stir in milk; bring to a boil. Cook and stir for 2 minutes. Remove from the heat. Stir in cheese until melted; set aside.

In a large skillet, saute mushrooms and onion in 2 tablespoons butter until tender. Add eggs and salt; cook and stir until the eggs are completely set. Add the cheese sauce and broccoli; mix well. Pour into a greased 11-in. x 7-in. x 2-in. baking dish.

Melt the remaining butter and toss with bread crumbs. Sprinkle over the egg mixture. Cover and refrigerate overnight.

Remove from refrigerator 30 minutes before baking. Bake, uncovered, at 350° for 25-30 minutes or until top is golden brown. **Yield:** 6-8 servings.

true belgian waffles

Rose Delemeester, St. Charles, Michigan

It was on a visit to my husband's relatives in Belgium that I was given this recipe. Back in the U.S., I served the waffles to his Belgian-born grandmother. She said they tasted just like home. The grandkids love these waffles almost anytime with about any kind of topping— blueberries, strawberries, raspberries, fried apples, powdered sugar or whipped topping.

      2 cups all-purpose flour
    3/4 cup sugar
3-1/2 teaspoons baking powder
      2 eggs, *separated*
  1-1/2 cups milk
      1 cup butter, melted
      1 teaspoon vanilla extract
Sliced fresh strawberries *or* syrup

In a bowl, combine flour, sugar and baking powder. In another bowl, lightly beat egg yolks. Add milk, butter and vanilla; mix well. Stir into the dry ingredients just until combined. Beat egg whites until stiff peaks form; fold into batter.

Bake in a preheated waffle iron according to manufacturer's directions until golden brown. Serve with strawberries or syrup. **Yield:** 10 waffles (about 4-1/2 inches).

amish baked oatmeal

Colleen Butler, Inwood, West Virginia
The first time I had this treat was at a bed-and-breakfast in Lancaster, Pennsylvania. To me, it tasted just like a big warm-from-the-oven oatmeal cookie! I'm a pastor's wife with three children. I make this oatmeal at home often at their request.

> **1-1/2 cups quick-cooking oats**
> **1/2 cup sugar**
> **1/2 cup milk**
> **1/4 cup butter, melted**
> **1 egg**
> **1 teaspoon baking powder**
> **3/4 teaspoon salt**
> **1 teaspoon vanilla extract**
> **Warm milk**
> **Fresh fruit, optional**
> **Brown sugar, optional**

Combine the first eight ingredients; mix well. Spread evenly in a greased 13-in. x 9-in. x 2-in. baking pan. Bake at 350° for 25-30 minutes or until edges are golden brown. Immediately spoon into bowls; add warm milk. Top with fresh fruit and/or brown sugar if desired. **Yield:** 6 servings.

herbed waffles with creamed beef

Lois McCormick, Muncy, Pennsylvania
This is a nice recipe to whip up when you come home from church. I adapted it from one I saw in an old cookbook. It's a little different way to use herbs.

> **2 cups all-purpose flour**
> **1 tablespoon baking powder**
> **1/2 teaspoon salt**
> **1-3/4 cups milk**
> **6 tablespoons butter, melted**
> **2 eggs, *separated***
> **1 tablespoon chopped fresh parsley**
> **1 tablespoon grated onion**
> **1/2 teaspoon rubbed sage**
> **1/2 teaspoon dried thyme**
> **CREAMED BEEF:**
> **6 tablespoons butter**
> **6 tablespoons all-purpose flour**
> **2-1/2 cups milk**
> **1/4 teaspoon dried thyme**
> **1 package (4 ounces) shredded dried beef**
> **Chopped fresh parsley, optional**

Combine the first three ingredients; set aside. In a mixing bowl, beat milk, butter, egg yolks, parsley, onion, sage and thyme. Gradually add dry ingredients; mix well. Beat egg whites until stiff peaks form; fold into batter. Bake in a preheated waffle iron according to manufacturer's directions until golden brown.

Meanwhile, in a saucepan, melt butter; add flour. Whisk in milk and thyme; bring to a boil. Cook and stir for 2 minutes or until thick. Add the beef and heat through. Serve over waffles. Sprinkle with parsley if desired. **Yield:** 7 waffles (6 inches).

sausage cheese braid

Christena Weed, Levant, Kansas

My husband and I have three married daughters, 10 grandchildren and four great-grandchildren—and they all like this. It's good for a snack anytime, too.

2 packages (1/4 ounce *each*) active dry yeast
1-1/4 cups warm water (110° to 115°)
2 tablespoons sugar
1-1/2 teaspoons salt
1 teaspoon Italian seasoning
2 eggs
1/4 cup butter, softened
4 to 4-1/2 cups all-purpose flour
1 pound bulk hot pork sausage
1 cup (4 ounces) shredded mozzarella *or* cheddar cheese

In a large mixing bowl, dissolve yeast in water. Add sugar, salt, Italian seasoning, 1 egg, butter and 2 cups flour; beat until smooth. Add enough remaining flour to form a soft dough.

Turn onto a floured surface; knead until smooth and elastic, about 6-8 minutes. Place in a greased bowl, turning once to grease top. Cover and let rise in a warm place until doubled, about 1 hour.

Meanwhile, in a skillet, cook sausage over medium heat until no longer pink; drain and set aside to cool. Punch the dough down; divide in half. On a floured surface, roll each half into a 14-in. x 12-in. rectangle. Cut each one into three 14-in. x 4-in. strips. Combine cheese and sausage; spoon 1/2 cup down the center of each strip. Bring long edges together over filling; pinch to seal. Place three strips with seam side down on greased baking sheets. Braid strips together; secure ends. Cover and let rise until doubled, about 45 minutes.

Beat remaining egg and brush over loaves. Bake at 400° for 20-25 minutes or until golden. Immediately remove from baking sheets to wire racks. Serve warm. **Yield:** 2 loaves.

★★★★★ prize winning tips

★ Turn plain smoked sausage into a breakfast treat by wrapping each slice with half of a bacon strip. Secure it with a toothpick, then place in a baking dish and sprinkle with brown sugar. Bake at 350° for 1 hour.

Julie Hinkenbein, Wentzville, Missouri

★ To add pizzazz to your buttermilk pancakes, spread each one with butter while still hot, then sprinkle with brown sugar and top with sliced bananas.

Shirley Noorlun, Battle Ground, Washington

★ When I make my cinnamon rolls, I find the easiest way to evenly cut them is to use unwaxed dental floss or thread. Simply place a 10-inch section of thread under the roll where you want to cut it. Bring the ends of the thread together and crisscross so that the thread cuts through the dough. Repeat until all of the rolls are cut.

Sandra Ziegel, Wausau, Wisconsin

creamed ham on toast

Robin Morton, Ripley, Mississippi
*Whether for breakfast or brunch—or lunch or supper—
this recipe has been popular in our family for years.
It is one that my grandmother passed down. Home
for my husband, me and our children, is a country town.
We love country life as well as country-style cooking.*

- 1 cup chopped fully cooked ham
- 1/3 cup chopped green pepper
- 1/4 cup sliced celery
- 2 tablespoons butter
- 3 tablespoons all-purpose flour
- 1-1/2 cups milk
- 1/4 teaspoon pepper
- 1/4 teaspoon celery seed
- 1 hard-cooked egg, chopped
- 5 slices process American cheese, cut into quarters
- 3 slices toast, cut into triangles

In a skillet, saute the ham, green pepper and celery in butter for 4-5 minutes or until tender. Sprinkle with flour; stir until smooth and bubbly. Add the milk, pepper and celery seed and bring to a boil. Cook and stir for 2 minutes.

Remove from the heat. Add egg and cheese; stir until cheese melts. Serve over toast. **Yield:** 2-3 servings.

apple nut hotcakes

Barbara Nowakowski, North Tonawanda, New York
*Not only are these an old family favorite, they're a
neighborhood favorite as well. We have several
bachelor neighbors who rave about them.*

- 1 cup all-purpose flour
- 2 tablespoons sugar
- 2 teaspoons baking powder
- 1/2 teaspoon salt
- 1/2 teaspoon ground cinnamon
- 3/4 cup milk
- 3 tablespoons butter, melted
- 2 teaspoons vanilla extract
- 2 egg whites
- 1/2 cup shredded peeled apple
- 1/2 cup chopped walnuts

APPLE SYRUP:
- 1/4 cup sugar
- 4 teaspoons cornstarch
- 1/4 teaspoon ground allspice
- 1-1/2 cups apple juice

In a large bowl, combine flour, sugar, baking powder, salt and cinnamon. In another bowl, combine milk, butter and vanilla; mix well. Stir into dry ingredients just until combined. Beat egg whites until stiff peaks form; fold into batter with apple and nuts.

Pour batter by 1/4 cupfuls onto a lightly greased hot griddle; turn when bubbles form on top. Cook until second side is golden brown.

For syrup, combine sugar, cornstarch and allspice in a medium saucepan; stir in apple juice. Cook and stir over medium heat until thickened, about 6-8 minutes. Serve over hotcakes. **Yield:** 10-12 hotcakes.

cinnamon swirl quick bread

Helen Richardson, Shelbyville, Michigan

When I was married over 30 years ago, I bought two popular cookbooks to learn the "basics." Now, I have over 2,000 cookbooks, booklets and recipe magazines. I take my bread—which I've been making for 20 years—to potlucks and parties. Plus, my family's always loved it.

- 1-1/2 cups sugar, *divided*
- 1 tablespoon ground cinnamon
- 2 cups all-purpose flour
- 1 teaspoon baking soda
- 1/2 teaspoon salt
- 1 cup buttermilk
- 1 egg
- 1/4 cup vegetable oil

GLAZE:
- 1/4 cup confectioners' sugar
- 1-1/2 to 2 teaspoons milk

Combine 1/2 cup sugar and cinnamon; set aside. Combine flour, baking soda, salt and remaining sugar. Combine buttermilk, egg and oil; stir into dry ingredients just until combined.

Grease the bottom only of a 9-in. x 5-in. x 3-in. loaf pan. Pour half of the batter into pan; sprinkle with half of the cinnamon-sugar. Carefully spread with remaining batter and sprinkle with remaining cinnamon-sugar; swirl knife through batter.

Bake at 350° for 45-50 minutes or until a toothpick inserted near the center comes out clean. Cool in pan 10 minutes before removing to a wire rack to cool completely. Combine glaze ingredients; drizzle over bread. **Yield:** 1 loaf.

morning orange drink

Joyce Mummau, Mt. Airy, Maryland

Although it requires only a few basic ingredients and little preparation, this drink always draws raves from overnight guests about its "wake-up" taste. We like it so much better than the flavor of store-bought orange juice.

- 1 can (6 ounces) frozen orange juice concentrate
- 1 cup cold water
- 1 cup milk
- 1/3 cup sugar
- 1 teaspoon vanilla extract
- 10 ice cubes

Combine the first five ingredients in a blender and process at high speed. Add ice cubes, a few at a time, blending until mixture is smooth. Serve immediately. **Yield:** 4-6 servings.

> *For a tasty change from plain oatmeal, I add chopped fresh peaches and a dash of cinnamon while cooking it. Apples and raisins are delicious additions, too.
> Paulette Reyenga, Brantford, Ontario

MEAT-AND-POTATO COMBOS

#1

BEEF STEW WITH
POTATO DUMPLINGS

beef stew with potato dumplings

T he dictionary may define meat and potatoes as "basic," but there's nothing ordinary about the winners of our Meat-and-Potato Combos contest! Plain and simple, they're all hearty good eating with a deliciously unexpected dash of pizzazz added.

"**Everyone who tries it** loves **this** flavorful **stew...**"

Pleasing pairings of beef, pork or poultry with potatoes had our panel of tasters smiling, nodding and asking for second helpings. Comparing notes on their favorites later, the judges easily agreed on a Grand Prize Winner—Beef Stew with Potato Dumplings from Shawn Asiala of Boca Raton, Florida.

Shawn's rich, meaty stew, topped with fluffy herb-flavored potato dumplings, is a stick-to-the-ribs feast impossible to resist. "Everyone who tries it loves this flavorful stew and asks me to share the recipe," says Shawn. "Sometimes, all I have to do is describe the stew and people ask for the recipe even before tasting it!"

1/4 cup all-purpose flour
3/4 teaspoon salt
1/2 teaspoon pepper
2 pounds beef stew meat, cubed
2 medium onions, chopped
2 tablespoons vegetable oil
2 cans (10-1/2 ounces *each*) condensed beef broth, undiluted
3/4 cup water
1 tablespoon red wine vinegar
6 medium carrots, cut into 2-inch chunks
2 bay leaves
1 teaspoon dried thyme
1/4 teaspoon garlic powder
DUMPLINGS:
1 egg
3/4 cup seasoned dry bread crumbs
1 tablespoon all-purpose flour
1 tablespoon minced fresh parsley
1 tablespoon minced onion
1/2 teaspoon dried thyme

1/2 teaspoon salt
1/2 teaspoon pepper
2-1/2 cups finely shredded raw potatoes
Additional all-purpose flour

In a plastic bag, combine flour, salt and pepper. Add meat; toss to coat. In a 4-qt. Dutch oven, cook meat and onions in oil until the meat is browned and onions are tender. Stir in broth, water, vinegar, carrots and seasonings; bring to a boil. Reduce heat; cover and simmer for 1-1/2 hours or until meat is almost tender. Remove bay leaves.

In a bowl, beat egg; add the bread crumbs, flour, parsley, onion and seasonings. Stir in potatoes; mix well. With floured hands, shape into 1-1/2-in. balls. Dust with flour.

Bring stew to a boil; drop dumplings onto stew. Cover and simmer for 30 minutes (do not lift cover) or until dumplings are done. Serve immediately. **Yield:** 6 servings.

hot german potato salad

Inez Senner, Glendive, Montana

I enjoy sharing favorite dishes at church and family potlucks. This one has won raves whenever I've served it. I've also found it makes a good lunch that's better the second time around!

- 9 medium potatoes
- 1-1/2 pounds fully cooked smoked sausage *or* precooked bratwurst
- 6 bacon strips
- 3/4 cup chopped onion
- 2 tablespoons all-purpose flour
- 1 teaspoon salt
- 1/2 teaspoon celery seed
- 1/8 teaspoon pepper
- 1/4 cup sugar
- 1-1/3 cups water
- 2/3 cup cider vinegar

In a saucepan, cook potatoes in boiling salted water until tender. Meanwhile, cut sausage into 1/2-in. slices; saute in a skillet until browned. Drain and place in a large bowl. Drain potatoes; peel and cut into 3/4-in. cubes. Add to sausage; keep warm.

Cook bacon until crisp; crumble and set aside. Drain all but 3 tablespoons of drippings; saute onion in drippings until tender. Stir in the flour, salt, celery seed and pepper; blend well. Add sugar, water and vinegar; bring to a boil. Boil for 2 minutes. Pour over potato mixture and stir gently to coat. Sprinkle with bacon. Serve warm. **Yield:** 12-14 servings.

meat loaf potato surprise

Lois Edwards, Citrus Heights, California

Although I'm retired after years of teaching school, my days continue to be full. So easy dishes like this still are a blessing to me.

- 1 cup soft bread crumbs
- 1/2 cup beef broth
- 1 egg, beaten
- 4 teaspoons dried minced onion
- 1 teaspoon salt
- 1/4 teaspoon Italian seasoning
- 1/4 teaspoon pepper
- 1-1/2 pounds ground beef
- 4 cups frozen shredded hash browns, thawed
- 1/3 cup grated Parmesan cheese
- 1/4 cup minced fresh parsley
- 1 teaspoon onion salt

SAUCE:
- 1 can (8 ounces) tomato sauce
- 1/4 cup beef broth
- 2 teaspoons prepared mustard

Additional Parmesan cheese, optional

In a bowl, combine bread crumbs, broth, egg and seasonings; let stand for 2 minutes. Add the beef and mix well. On a piece of waxed paper, pat meat mixture into a 10-in. square.

Combine hash browns, cheese, parsley and onion salt; spoon over meat. Roll up jelly-roll style, removing waxed paper as you roll. Pinch edges and ends to seal; place with seam side down in an ungreased shallow baking pan.

Bake at 375° for 40 minutes. Combine the first three sauce ingredients; spoon over meat loaf. Return to the oven for 10 minutes. Sprinkle with Parmesan cheese if desired. **Yield:** 8 servings.

roast pork and potatoes

Denise Collins, Chillicothe, Ohio

We used to raise our own hogs. This recipe was given to me by a fellow farmer who also had pork on the dinner table a couple of times a week. I'm a dietitian at the local VA hospital. Cooking, of course, is one of my top pastimes!

- 1 envelope onion soup mix
- 2 garlic cloves, minced
- 1 tablespoon dried rosemary, crushed
- 1/2 teaspoon salt
- 1/2 teaspoon pepper
- 1/4 teaspoon ground cloves
- 3 cups water, *divided*
- 1 pork loin roast with bone (4 to 5 pounds)
- 24 small red potatoes, halved (2 to 3 pounds)
- 1-1/2 cups sliced onions

In a bowl, combine the first six ingredients. Stir in 1/2 cup water; let stand for 3 minutes. Place roast, fat side up, on a greased rack in a roasting pan. Pour remaining water into the pan. Combine potatoes and onions; spoon around the roast. Brush vegetables and roast with seasoning mixture.

Bake, uncovered, at 325° for 2-1/2 to 3 hours or until a meat thermometer reads 160°-170° and potatoes are tender. Baste and stir potatoes occasionally. Tent with foil if browning too fast. Thicken juices for gravy if desired. Let stand 10 minutes before slicing. **Yield:** 8-10 servings.

beef and potato boats

Linda Wheeler, Harrisburg, Pennsylvania

Back when I was teaching elementary school (I'm now a busy stay-at-home mom), my class would put together a Mother's Day cookbook. Many of the dishes are still my favorites—this one included.

- 4 large baking potatoes (8 to 10 ounces *each*)
- 2 tablespoons butter
- 1-1/4 teaspoons salt, *divided*
- Dash pepper
- 1/4 to 1/3 cup milk
- 1 pound ground beef
- 1 small onion, chopped
- 6 bacon strips, cooked and crumbled
- 1/2 cup sour cream
- 1/4 cup shredded cheddar cheese

Wash potato skins and prick with a fork. Bake at 400° for 60-70 minutes or until tender. Allow potatoes to cool to the touch. Slice a small portion off the top of each potato. Carefully scoop out the pulp, leaving a 1/4-in. shell. In a bowl, mash the pulp with butter, 1/2 teaspoon salt, pepper and milk; set aside.

In a saucepan over medium heat, cook the beef and onion until meat is no longer pink; drain. Cool 10 minutes. Add bacon, sour cream and remaining salt. Spoon into potato shells. Top each with a fourth of the mashed potato mixture; sprinkle with cheese.

Place potatoes on an ungreased baking sheet. Bake at 400° for 20-25 minutes or until heated through. **Yield:** 4 servings.

chicken potato bake

Myrtle Nelson, Wetaskiwin, Alberta

When I came up with this recipe, I was looking for something that didn't require last-minute fuss. It's great getting compliments on something so simple!

- 1 cup dry bread crumbs
- 1/2 cup all-purpose flour
- 2 teaspoons salt
- 2 teaspoons paprika
- 1 teaspoon seasoned salt
- 1 teaspoon sugar
- 1 teaspoon onion powder
- 1 teaspoon rubbed sage
- 1 teaspoon dried oregano
- 1/2 teaspoon pepper
- 1/2 teaspoon celery seed
- 1/2 teaspoon dried parsley flakes
- 1/4 teaspoon garlic powder
- 3-1/2 to 4 pounds chicken pieces, skin removed
- 3 tablespoons vegetable oil

POTATOES:

- 1 teaspoon vegetable oil
- 1 teaspoon seasoned salt
- 1 teaspoon dried parsley flakes
- 1/2 teaspoon paprika
- 1/8 teaspoon garlic powder
- 1/8 teaspoon pepper
- 4 medium red potatoes, cut into 1-inch cubes

In a shallow bowl, combine the first 13 ingredients. Dip chicken in oil; coat with crumb mixture. Place on a greased 15-in. x 10-in. x 1-in. baking pan.

For potatoes, combine oil, salt, parsley, paprika, garlic powder and pepper in a bowl. Add potatoes; stir until coated. Place around chicken. Bake, uncovered, at 350° for 1 hour or until potatoes are tender and chicken juices run clear. **Yield:** 4 servings.

potato lasagna

Mara Beaumont, South Milwaukee, Wisconsin

At our house, this is a regular—it's as much fun to fix as it is to eat! It's great for potlucks as well.

- 2 tablespoons olive oil
- 2 garlic cloves, minced
- 1/2 teaspoon *each* salt and pepper
- 7 medium potatoes, sliced 1/4 inch thick
- 1 pound bulk Italian sausage
- 1 large onion, chopped
- 2 packages (10 ounces *each*) frozen chopped spinach, thawed and drained
- 1 cup ricotta cheese
- 1/4 cup Italian-seasoned dry bread crumbs

Dash cayenne pepper

Additional salt and pepper to taste

- 2 cups (8 ounces) shredded mozzarella cheese
- 1/2 cup chicken broth
- 2 tablespoons grated Parmesan cheese

In a large bowl, combine oil, garlic, salt and pepper. Add the potatoes and toss to coat; spread evenly in an ungreased 15-in. x 10-in. x 1-in. baking pan. Cover tightly with foil. Bake at 425° for 35-40 minutes or until tender. Cool at least 15 minutes.

Meanwhile, in a large skillet, cook sausage and onion over medium heat until no longer pink; drain. Combine spinach, ricotta, crumbs, cayenne, salt and pepper.

Arrange a third of the potatoes evenly in a greased 13-in. x 9-in. x 2-in. baking dish. Layer with half of the spinach mixture, half of the sausage and half of the mozzarella. Repeat with a third of the potatoes and the remaining spinach mixture, sausage and mozzarella. Pour broth over all. Top with remaining potatoes; sprinkle with Parmesan. Bake, uncovered, at 350° for 30-35 minutes. Let stand 5 minutes before serving. **Yield:** 8-10 servings.

runners-up

herbed cornish pasties

Maribeth Edwards, Follansbee, West Virginia
These hand-held golden pockets are packed with the irresistible combination of beef and potatoes.

2 cups all-purpose flour
1 teaspoon salt
1/2 teaspoon *each* dried basil and thyme
1/2 cup shortening
1/4 cup butter
5 to 6 tablespoons ice water

FILLING:
1 pound boneless beef chuck, cut
   into 1/2-inch cubes
2 tablespoons vegetable oil, *divided*
1 teaspoon salt
1/8 teaspoon pepper
2 tablespoons all-purpose flour
1 cup water
2 medium potatoes, peeled and diced
1/2 cup *each* diced carrot and onion
1 egg, lightly beaten

In a bowl, combine flour, salt, basil and thyme; cut in shortening and butter until crumbly. Add water, 1 tablespoon at a time, tossing lightly with a fork until mixture forms a ball. Cover and chill for at least 30 minutes.

Meanwhile, brown beef in a skillet in 1 tablespoon oil; sprinkle with salt and pepper. Remove with a slotted spoon; set aside. Add remaining oil to skillet; gradually stir in flour until smooth. Cook and stir over medium heat for about 2-3 minutes or until lightly browned. Gradually add water; whisk until smooth.

Return beef to skillet. Reduce heat; cover and simmer for 20 minutes. Add potatoes, carrot and onion. Cover and simmer for 25 minutes or until tender. Remove from the heat; cool.

Divide pastry into four equal portions. On a lightly floured surface, roll out one portion into a 9-in. circle. Mound 3/4 cup filling on half of circle. Moisten edges with water; fold dough over filling and press edges with a fork to seal. Place on an ungreased baking sheet. Repeat with remaining pastry and filling. Cut three slits in top of each; brush with egg. Bake at 400° for 25-30 minutes or until golden brown. **Yield:** 4 servings.

---

prize winning tips

✱For a hearty but quick one-pot dinner, spread four or five medium sliced potatoes over the bottom of a large saucepan. Lightly salt and top with a pound of hamburger made into a large patty the size of the pan lid. Add a sliced onion and two or three sliced carrots. Cover and cook on low for 1 hour.

Marj Ridgeway, Brashear, Texas

✱When I'm in a hurry, I make hash by browning a package of smoked sausage, a small onion and six sliced potatoes in a little oil.

Donna Brandt, Churubusco, Indiana

shepherd's pie

Diane Gillingham, Carman, Manitoba
As the second oldest of eight children in a farm family, I had plenty of opportunity to cook while I was growing up. For "country eaters," this hearty pie is perfect!

       1 pound ground beef
     3/4 cup chopped onion
       2 garlic cloves, minced
       3 tablespoons vegetable oil, *divided*
       1 cup chopped fresh mushrooms
       1 tablespoon tomato paste
     1/2 cup beef broth
       2 teaspoons prepared horseradish
       1 teaspoon ground mustard
   1-1/2 teaspoons salt, *divided*
     1/4 teaspoon pepper
     1/2 cup diced green pepper
     1/2 cup diced sweet red pepper
       8 medium potatoes, peeled and cubed
     1/3 cup hot milk
       1 cup (4 ounces) shredded cheddar cheese
       2 egg whites

In a skillet, cook beef, onion and garlic in 2 tablespoons of oil. Add mushrooms. Cook and stir for 3 minutes; drain. Place tomato paste in a bowl. Gradually whisk in broth until smooth. Stir in horseradish, mustard, 1 teaspoon salt and pepper. Add to meat mixture. Pour into a greased 11-in. x 7-in. x 2-in. baking pan; set aside.

In same skillet, saute peppers in remaining oil until tender, about 3 minutes. Drain and spoon over meat mixture.

Cook potatoes in boiling salted water until tender; drain. Mash with milk, cheese and remaining salt. Beat egg whites until stiff peaks form; gently fold into potatoes. Spoon over pepper layer. Bake, uncovered, at 425° for 15 minutes. Reduce heat to 350°; bake 20 minutes longer or until meat layer is bubbly. **Yield:** 4-6 servings.

steak potpie

Pattie Bonner, Cocoa, Florida
When I hear "meat and potatoes," this is the recipe that immediately comes to mind. I've made it for years.

     3/4 cup sliced onions
       4 tablespoons vegetable oil, *divided*
     1/4 cup all-purpose flour
       1 teaspoon salt
     1/2 teaspoon pepper
     1/2 teaspoon paprika
   Pinch *each* ground allspice and ginger
       1 pound boneless round steak, cut
          into 1/2-inch pieces
   2-1/2 cups boiling water
       3 medium potatoes, peeled and diced
   Pastry for single-crust pie

In a large skillet, saute the onions in 2 tablespoons oil until golden. Drain and set aside. In a plastic bag, combine dry ingredients; add meat and shake to coat. Brown meat in remaining oil in the same skillet. Add water; cover and simmer until meat is tender, about 1 hour. Add potatoes; simmer, uncovered, for 15-20 minutes or until the potatoes are tender. Pour into a greased 1-1/2-qt. baking dish. Top with onion slices.

Roll pastry to fit baking dish. Place over hot filling; seal to edges of dish. Make slits in the crust. Bake at 450° for 25-30 minutes or until golden brown. If necessary, cover edges of crust with foil to prevent overbrowning. **Yield:** 4-6 servings.

chicken with potato stuffing

Carla Kreider, Quarryville, Pennsylvania
This is a great Sunday meal or company dish—as long as you're prepared with second helpings!

6 medium red potatoes, cut into 1-inch cubes
1 pound Italian sausage
1 cup finely chopped onion
1 tablespoon butter
4 teaspoons dried parsley flakes, *divided*
1 teaspoon salt
3/4 teaspoon dried rosemary, crushed
2-3/4 teaspoons dried thyme, *divided*
1/2 teaspoon pepper
1 roasting chicken (7 to 7-1/2 pounds)
1 tablespoon vegetable oil
1 cup water

Cook potatoes in boiling salted water until almost tender; drain and set aside. Cook sausage in boiling water for 10 minutes; drain. Halve each sausage lengthwise, then cut into 1/2-in. pieces.

In a large skillet over medium heat, cook potatoes, sausage and onion in butter until sausage is browned and onion is tender. Add 2 teaspoons parsley, salt, rosemary, 3/4 teaspoon thyme and pepper.

Stuff chicken. Place remaining stuffing in a greased 1-1/2-qt. baking dish; cover and refrigerate. Place chicken in a roasting pan; brush with oil and sprinkle with remaining parsley and thyme. Add water to pan. Bake, uncovered, at 350° for 1-1/2 hours.

Place baking dish of stuffing in oven. Bake chicken and stuffing for 45 minutes or until a meat thermometer reads 180°. Thicken drippings if desired. **Yield:** 8 servings.

ham 'n' spuds salad

Jo Baker, Litchfield, Illinois
Not only does this make a hearty salad that's a favorite of men and good for carrying to picnics and church suppers…it's also a tasty way to use up ham!

2 cups cubed cooked potatoes
2 cups cubed fully cooked ham
4 hard-cooked eggs, chopped
1/2 cup pitted ripe olives
1/2 cup sliced celery
1/4 cup finely chopped green pepper
1/4 cup finely chopped onion
1/2 cup mayonnaise
1/4 cup sweet pickle relish
2 tablespoons minced pimientos
1 tablespoon prepared spicy brown *or* yellow mustard
2 teaspoons cider vinegar
Lettuce leaves, optional

In a bowl, combine potatoes, ham, eggs, olives, celery, green pepper and onion. In a small bowl, combine mayonnaise, relish, pimientos, mustard and vinegar; pour over potato mixture. Toss lightly to coat. Chill for several hours. Serve in a lettuce-lined bowl if desired. **Yield:** 6-8 servings.

CHICKEN RECIPES

1

NUTTY OVEN-FRIED
CHICKEN

nutty oven-fried chicken

Choosing a winner in *Taste of Home's* first-ever national recipe contest—Chicken Recipes held in 1993—was quite a challenge. Nearly 1,000 home-style recipes were entered by great home cooks from coast to coast.

"...the chicken comes out so moist, tasty and crispy."

Our panel of judges spent weeks narrowing the pleasing poultry selection to a few dozen of the most promising entries, which were then carefully prepared and enthusiastically taste-tested.

When the votes were finally tallied, the Grand Prize was awarded to Diane Hixon of Niceville, Florida for her Nutty Oven-Fried Chicken, picked the fairest of the fowl.

"The pecans that give this dish its unique nutty flavor are plentiful in the South, and so is chicken," says Diane. "I love to make and serve this easy dish because the chicken comes out so moist, tasty and crispy."

1 **cup biscuit/baking mix**
1/3 **cup finely chopped pecans**
2 **teaspoons paprika**
1/2 **teaspoon salt**
1/2 **teaspoon poultry seasoning**
1/2 **teaspoon rubbed sage**
1 **broiler-fryer chicken (2 to 3 pounds), cut up**
1/2 **cup evaporated milk**
1/3 **cup butter, melted**

In a shallow dish, combine biscuit mix, pecans and seasonings; mix well. Dip chicken pieces in milk; coat generously with pecan mixture.

Place in a lightly greased 13-in. x 9-in. x 2-in. baking dish. Drizzle butter over chicken. Bake, uncovered, at 350° for 1 hour or until juices run clear. **Yield:** 6-8 servings.

chicken chili with black beans

Jeanette Urbom, Overland Park, Kansas
Because this dish looks different from traditional chili, my family was a little hesitant to try it at first. But thanks to full, hearty flavor, it's become a real favorite around our house. I like to serve it with warm corn bread.

- 3 whole boneless skinless chicken breasts (about 1-3/4 pounds), cubed
- 2 medium sweet red peppers, chopped
- 1 large onion, chopped
- 4 garlic cloves, minced
- 3 tablespoons olive oil
- 1 can (4 ounces) chopped green chilies
- 2 tablespoons chili powder
- 2 teaspoons ground cumin
- 1 teaspoon ground coriander
- 2 cans (15 ounces *each*) black beans, rinsed and drained
- 1 can (28 ounces) Italian plum tomatoes, chopped, undrained
- 1 cup chicken broth *or* beer

In a Dutch oven, saute chicken, red peppers, onion and garlic in oil for 5 minutes or until chicken is no longer pink. Add green chilies, chili powder, cumin and coriander; cook for 3 minutes.

Stir in beans, tomatoes and broth or beer; bring to a boil. Reduce heat and simmer, uncovered, for 15 minutes, stirring often. **Yield:** 10 servings (3 quarts).

chicken fajitas

Lindsay St. John, Plainfield, Indiana
Fresh flavor with a flair describes this quick and easy recipe. Fajitas are great for hot summer evenings when you want to serve something fun and tasty, yet keep cooking to a minimum. Try topping them with sour cream, guacamole or both. My family loves them!

- 1/4 cup lime juice
- 1 garlic clove, minced
- 1 teaspoon chili powder
- 1/2 teaspoon ground cumin
- 2 whole boneless skinless chicken breasts, cut into strips
- 1 medium onion, cut into thin wedges
- 1/2 medium sweet red pepper, cut into strips
- 1/2 medium yellow pepper, cut into strips
- 1/2 medium green pepper, cut into strips
- 1/2 cup salsa
- 12 flour tortillas (8 inches)
- 1-1/2 cups (6 ounces) shredded cheddar *or* Monterey Jack cheese

In a small bowl, combine lime juice, garlic, chili powder and cumin. Add chicken; stir. Marinate for 15 minutes.

In a nonstick skillet, cook onion, chicken and marinade for 3 minutes or until chicken is no longer pink. Add peppers; saute for 3-5 minutes or until crisp-tender. Stir in salsa. Divide mixture among tortillas; top with cheese. Roll up and serve. **Yield:** 6 servings.

barbecued chicken

Linda Scott, Hahira, Georgia

I adapted my mother's recipe for barbecue sauce to suit our tastes. Every summer, we have a neighborhood cookout. I take this chicken and watch it disappear!

>   2 broiler-fryer chickens (2 to 3 pounds *each*), cut up

SEASONING MIX:

>   3 tablespoons salt
>   2 tablespoons onion powder
>   1 tablespoon paprika
>   2 teaspoons garlic powder
> 1-1/2 teaspoons chili powder
> 1-1/2 teaspoons pepper
>   1/4 teaspoon ground turmeric

Pinch ground red pepper

SAUCE:

>   2 cups ketchup
>   3 tablespoons brown sugar
>   2 tablespoons dried minced onion
>   2 tablespoons frozen orange juice concentrate, thawed
>   1 tablespoon Seasoning Mix (recipe above)
>   1/2 teaspoon Liquid Smoke, optional

Pat chicken pieces dry so seasoning coats well; set aside. Combine seasoning mix ingredients; sprinkle over both sides of the chicken. Reserve 1 tablespoon mix for sauce. Store leftovers in a covered container.

Grill chicken, skin side down, uncovered, over medium heat for 20 minutes. Turn; grill 20-30 minutes more or until chicken is tender and no longer pink. Meanwhile, combine sauce ingredients in a small bowl. During the last 10 minutes of grilling, brush chicken often with sauce. **Yield:** 12 servings.

chinese chicken salad

Shirley Smith, Yorba Linda, California

Here's a cool, easy entree perfect for steamy summer days! You can do most of the preparation for this dish ahead of time and just mix it together before serving. The crispy lettuce and wonton strips keep this dish light, while the chicken and dressing give it wonderful flavor.

>   1/2 package wonton wrappers, cut into 1/4-inch strips

Oil for deep-fat frying

>   3 cups cubed cooked chicken
>   1 head lettuce, shredded
>   4 green onions with tops, sliced
>   4 tablespoons sesame seeds, toasted

DRESSING:

>   1/3 cup white wine vinegar
>   1/4 cup sugar
>   3 tablespoons vegetable oil
>   2 tablespoons sesame oil
>   1 teaspoon salt
>   1/2 teaspoon pepper

Deep-fry wonton strips in oil until brown and crisp. Drain on paper towels; set aside. In a large salad bowl, combine chicken, lettuce, green onions and sesame seeds.

In a small bowl, whisk together all of the dressing ingredients. Just before serving, add fried wonton strips to salad; pour dressing over and toss to coat. **Yield:** 6-8 servings.

Editor's Note: For faster preparation, a can of chow mein noodles can be substituted for the wonton strips.

artichoke chicken

Ruth Stenson, Santa Ana, California
Rosemary, mushrooms and artichokes combine to give chicken a wonderful, savory flavor. It's always a big hit with everyone—especially my family!

    8 boneless skinless chicken breast halves
    2 tablespoons butter
    2 jars (6 ounces *each*) marinated artichoke
      hearts, drained
    1 jar (4-1/2 ounces) whole mushrooms, drained
    1/2 cup chopped onion
    1/3 cup all-purpose flour
    1-1/2 teaspoons dried rosemary
    1 teaspoon salt
    1/4 teaspoon pepper
    2 cups chicken broth *or* 1 cup broth and 1 cup
      dry white wine
Hot cooked noodles
Chopped fresh parsley

In a skillet, brown chicken in butter. Remove chicken to an ungreased 13-in. x 9-in. x 2-in. baking dish; do not drain pan juices. Cut the artichokes into quarters. Arrange artichokes and mushrooms on top of chicken; set aside.

Saute onion in pan juices; blend in flour, rosemary, salt and pepper. Add chicken broth; cook until thickened and bubbly. Remove from heat; spoon over chicken.

Cover and bake at 350° for 50-60 minutes or until chicken is tender. Place noodles on serving platter; top with chicken and sauce. Sprinkle with parsley. **Yield:** 8 servings.

chicken tetrazzini

Kelly Heusmann, Cincinnati, Ohio
My husband is not a casserole lover, but this creamy, cheesy dish is one of his favorites! Nutmeg gives it a wonderful, different taste.

    2 cups sliced mushrooms
    1/4 cup butter
    1/4 cup all-purpose flour
    2 cups chicken broth
    1/4 cup half-and-half cream
    1 tablespoon chopped fresh parsley
    1 teaspoon salt
    1/8 to 1/4 teaspoon ground nutmeg
    1/4 teaspoon pepper
    3 tablespoons dry white wine *or* additional
      chicken broth
    3 cups cubed cooked chicken
    8 ounces spaghetti, cooked and drained
    3/4 cup shredded Parmesan cheese
Additional parsley

In a skillet, cook mushrooms in butter until tender. Stir in flour; gradually add the chicken broth. Cook, stirring constantly, until sauce comes to a boil. Remove from the heat; stir in cream, parsley, salt, nutmeg, pepper and wine or additional broth. Fold in the chicken and spaghetti.

Turn into a greased 12-in. x 8-in. x 2-in. baking dish; sprinkle with Parmesan cheese. Bake, uncovered, at 350° for 30 minutes or until heated through. Garnish with parsley. **Yield:** 8 servings.

chicken cheese lasagna

Mary Ann Kosmas, Minneapolis, Minnesota
This creamy pasta dish gives an old favorite a new twist!
Three cheeses and chicken blended with the fresh taste of
spinach make it a real crowd-pleaser. Try it served with a
green salad and a light dessert.

- 1 medium onion, chopped
- 1 garlic clove, minced
- 1/2 cup butter
- 1/2 cup all-purpose flour
- 1 teaspoon salt
- 2 cups chicken broth
- 1-1/2 cups milk
- 4 cups (16 ounces) shredded mozzarella cheese, *divided*
- 1 cup grated Parmesan cheese, *divided*
- 1 teaspoon dried basil
- 1 teaspoon dried oregano
- 1/2 teaspoon white pepper
- 2 cups ricotta cheese
- 1 tablespoon minced fresh parsley
- 9 lasagna noodles (8 ounces), cooked and drained
- 2 packages (10 ounces *each*) frozen spinach, thawed and well drained
- 2 cups cubed cooked chicken

In a saucepan, saute the onion and garlic in butter until tender. Stir in the flour and salt; cook until bubbly. Gradually stir in the broth and milk. Bring to a boil, stirring constantly. Boil 1 minute. Stir in 2 cups mozzarella cheese, 1/2 cup Parmesan cheese, basil, oregano and pepper; set aside.

In a bowl, combine ricotta cheese, parsley and remaining mozzarella; set aside.

Spread one-quarter of the cheese sauce into a greased 13-in. x 9-in. x 2-in. baking dish; cover with one-third of the noodles. Top with half of ricotta mixture, half of spinach and half of chicken. Cover with one-quarter of cheese sauce and one-third of noodles. Repeat layers of ricotta mixture, spinach, chicken and one-quarter cheese sauce. Cover with remaining noodles and cheese sauce. Sprinkle remaining Parmesan cheese over all. Bake at 350°, uncovered, for 35-40 minutes. Let stand 15 minutes. **Yield:** 12 servings.

---

prize winning tips

* ✱ Chicken is easier to cut into strips if it's semi-frozen.

  Amy Wolfe, Kittanning, Pennsylvania

* ✱ A fresh lemon makes a nice rub for a whole chicken. Then simply add a dusting of sage.

  Anna Moore, Howell, New Jersey

* ✱ When making your favorite coating mix for chicken, double or triple the amount and store the extra in resealable plastic bags.

  Opal Bobo, Cincinnati, Ohio

cashew chicken

Ena Quiggle, Goodhue, Minnesota
We love eating ethnic foods, especially Oriental dishes. This chicken stir-fry is my family's favorite! The cashews add crunch and a sweet, nutty flavor, and the tasty sauce adds richness to garden-fresh carrots and broccoli.

   1 tablespoon sesame oil
 1/4 cup rice wine vinegar
 1/4 cup sherry *or* 3 tablespoons chicken broth
      plus 1 tablespoon apple juice
   1 teaspoon garlic powder
1-1/2 pounds boneless skinless chicken, cubed
   3 tablespoons vegetable oil
   3 cups broccoli florets
   1 cup thinly sliced carrots
   2 teaspoons cornstarch
 1/3 cup soy sauce
 1/3 cup hoisin sauce
   1 tablespoon ground ginger
   1 cup roasted salted cashews
Hot cooked rice

In a large bowl, combine first four ingredients; add chicken and toss to coat. Cover and refrigerate for 2 hours.

Remove chicken from marinade and reserve marinade. Heat oil in a wok or large skillet. Stir-fry chicken for 2-3 minutes or until it is no longer pink. With a slotted spoon, remove chicken and set aside.

In the same skillet, stir-fry broccoli and carrots for 3 minutes or just until crisp-tender. Combine cornstarch, soy sauce, hoisin sauce, ginger and reserved marinade; stir into vegetables. Cook and stir until slightly thickened and bubbly. Stir in cashews and chicken; heat through. Serve over rice. **Yield:** 6 servings.

sweet gingered chicken wings

Debbie Dougal, Roseville, California
I first tasted this delicious chicken dish years ago when I attended a class on using honey in cooking. When I prepare this recipe for a party, it's one of the first dishes to disappear.

 1 cup all-purpose flour
 2 teaspoons salt
 2 teaspoons paprika
1/4 teaspoon pepper
24 chicken wings
SAUCE:
1/4 cup honey
1/4 cup frozen orange juice concentrate, thawed
1/2 teaspoon ground ginger
Snipped fresh parsley, optional

In a bowl, combine flour, salt, paprika and pepper. Coat chicken wings in flour mixture; shake off excess. Place wings on a large greased baking sheet. Bake at 350° for 30 minutes. Remove from the oven and drain.

Combine honey, orange juice concentrate and ginger; brush generously over chicken wings. Reduce heat to 325°.

Bake for 30-40 minutes or until chicken tests done, basting occasionally with more sauce. Sprinkle with parsley before serving if desired. **Yield:** 2 dozen.

phyllo chicken

Joyce Mummau, Mt. Airy, Maryland
Some years ago I found this recipe and streamlined it to fit our family. The broccoli adds a lot to the rich flavor. Phyllo is fun to work with, and its flakiness turns standard ingredients into a special, satisfying entree.

- 1/2 cup butter, melted, *divided*
- 12 sheets phyllo pastry dough
- 3 cups diced cooked chicken
- 1/2 pound bacon, cooked and crumbled
- 1 package (10 ounces) frozen chopped broccoli, thawed and drained
- 2 cups (8 ounces) shredded cheddar *or* Swiss cheese
- 6 eggs
- 1 cup half-and-half cream *or* evaporated milk
- 1/2 cup milk
- 1 teaspoon salt
- 1/2 teaspoon pepper

Brush sides and bottom of a 13-in. x 9-in. x 2-in. baking dish with some of the melted butter. Place one sheet of phyllo in bottom of dish; brush with butter. Repeat with five more sheets of phyllo. (Keep remaining phyllo dough covered with waxed paper to avoid drying out.)

In a bowl, combine chicken, bacon, broccoli and cheese; spread evenly over phyllo in baking dish. In another bowl, whisk together eggs, cream, milk, salt and pepper; pour over chicken mixture.

Cover filling with one sheet of phyllo; brush with butter. Repeat with remaining phyllo dough. Brush top with remaining butter. Bake, uncovered, at 375° for 35-40 minutes or until a knife inserted near the center comes out clean. **Yield:** 10-12 servings.

cheesy chicken chowder

Hazel Fritchie, Palestine, Illinois
I like to serve this hearty chowder with garlic bread and a salad. It's a wonderful dish to prepare when company drops in. The rich, mild flavor and tender chicken and vegetables appeal even to children and picky eaters.

- 3 cups chicken broth
- 2 cups diced peeled potatoes
- 1 cup diced carrots
- 1 cup diced celery
- 1/2 cup diced onion
- 1-1/2 teaspoons salt
- 1/4 teaspoon pepper
- 1/4 cup butter
- 1/3 cup all-purpose flour
- 2 cups milk
- 2 cups (8 ounces) shredded cheddar cheese
- 2 cups diced cooked chicken

In a 4-qt. saucepan, bring chicken broth to a boil. Reduce heat; add potatoes, carrots, celery, onion, salt and pepper. Cover and simmer for 15 minutes or until vegetables are tender.

Meanwhile, melt butter in a medium saucepan; add flour and mix well. Gradually stir in milk; cook over low heat until slightly thickened. Stir in cheese and cook until melted; add to broth along with chicken. Cook and stir over low heat until heated through. **Yield:** 6-8 servings.

runners-up

GROUND BEEF ROUNDUP #1

MEATBALL PIE

Mention meatballs, and most folks think of spaghetti. Sure enough, there were some super sauces entered in our Ground Beef Roundup contest. There were other delicious meatball dishes as well.

It was a meatball pie, however, that caught our judges' eyes and tantalized their taste buds the most.

"The combination of tomatoes, carrots and peas is colorful and appetizing."

After sampling dozens of different ground beef dishes, they awarded the Grand Prize to Susan Keith of Fort Plain, New York for her hearty and satisfying Meatball Pie.

"Meatball Pie looks as good as it tastes," says Susan. "The combination of tomatoes, carrots and peas is colorful and appetizing—so pretty on the table as a meal with a salad or coleslaw as a side dish.

"My roots in New England are likely what sparked my fondness for meat pies," she concludes. "I make pies with everything from chicken and pork to tuna."

3/4 cup soft bread crumbs
1/4 cup chopped onion
2 tablespoons minced fresh parsley
1 teaspoon salt
1/2 teaspoon dried marjoram
1/8 teaspoon pepper
1/4 cup milk
1 egg, lightly beaten
1 pound ground beef
1 can (14-1/2 ounces) stewed tomatoes
1 tablespoon cornstarch
2 teaspoons beef bouillon granules
1 cup frozen peas
1 cup sliced carrots, cooked
CRUST:
2-2/3 cups all-purpose flour
1/2 teaspoon salt
1 cup shortening
7 to 8 tablespoons ice water
Half-and-half cream

In a bowl, combine the first eight ingredients; crumble beef over mixture and mix well (mixture will be soft). Divide into fourths; shape each portion into 12 small meatballs. Brown meatballs, a few at a time, in a large skillet; drain and set aside.

Drain tomatoes, reserving liquid. Combine the liquid with cornstarch; pour into the skillet. Add tomatoes and bouillon; bring to a boil over medium heat, stirring constantly. Stir in peas and carrots. Remove from the heat and set aside.

For crust, combine flour and salt in a bowl. Cut in shortening until the mixture resembles coarse crumbs. Add water, 1 tablespoon at a time, tossing lightly with a fork until dough forms a ball.

On a lightly floured surface, roll half of dough to fit a 10-in. pie plate. Place in ungreased plate; add meatballs. Spoon tomato mixture over top. Roll remaining pastry to fit top of pie. Place over filling; seal and flute edges. Cut vents in top crust. Brush with cream.

Bake at 400° for 45-50 minutes or until golden brown. If needed, cover edges with foil for the last 10 minutes to prevent overbrowning. Let stand for 10 minutes before cutting. **Yield:** 6 servings.

spaghetti 'n' meatballs

Mary Lou Koskella, Prescott, Arizona
One evening, we had unexpected company. Since I had some of these meatballs left over in the freezer, I warmed them up as appetizers. Everyone raved!

1-1/2 cups chopped onion
 3 garlic cloves, minced
 2 tablespoons vegetable oil
 3 cups water
 1 can (29 ounces) tomato sauce
 2 cans (12 ounces *each*) tomato paste
 1/3 cup minced fresh parsley
 1 tablespoon dried basil
 1 tablespoon salt
 1/2 teaspoon pepper
MEATBALLS:
 4 eggs, lightly beaten
 2 cups soft bread cubes (1/4-inch pieces)
1-1/2 cups milk
 1 cup grated Parmesan cheese
 3 garlic cloves, minced
 1 tablespoon salt
 1/2 teaspoon pepper
 3 pounds ground beef
 2 tablespoons vegetable oil
Hot cooked spaghetti

In a Dutch oven over medium heat, saute onion and garlic in oil. Add water, tomato sauce and paste, parsley, basil, salt and pepper; bring to a boil. Reduce heat; cover and simmer for 50 minutes.

Combine the first seven meatball ingredients; crumble beef over mixture and mix well. Shape into 1-1/2-in. balls. In a skillet over medium heat, brown meatballs in oil; drain. Add to sauce; bring to a boil. Reduce heat; cover and simmer for 1 hour, stirring occasionally. Serve over spaghetti. **Yield:** 12-16 servings.

crispy beef tostadas

Joy Rackham, Chimacum, Washington
This one-dish ground beef meal I created myself is a family favorite.

 3 cups all-purpose flour
 5 teaspoons baking powder
1-1/4 cups milk
 1 pound ground beef
 2 garlic cloves, minced
 1 can (4 ounces) chopped green chilies
 1 envelope taco seasoning mix
 3/4 cup water
 1 can (16 ounces) refried beans
Oil for deep-fat frying
Picante sauce *or* salsa, shredded lettuce, finely chopped green onions, diced tomatoes and shredded cheddar cheese

In a large bowl, combine flour and baking powder; add the milk to form a soft dough. Cover and let rest for 1 hour. About 30 minutes before serving, cook beef and garlic in a skillet until meat is no longer pink; drain. Stir in chilies, taco seasoning and water; simmer for 10 minutes. Stir in beans; heat through and keep warm.

Divide dough into sixths. On a lightly floured surface, roll each portion into a 7-in. circle. In a deep-fat fryer, preheat oil to 375°. Fry tostadas in hot oil until golden, turning once; drain on paper towels.

Top each with meat mixture, picante sauce or salsa, lettuce, onions, tomatoes and cheese; serve immediately. **Yield:** 6 servings.

chili with potato dumplings

Shirley Marshall, Michigantown, Indiana
Now that my husband has retired, we eat out a lot. If we stay home, though, he asks if we can have this chili!

- 1 pound ground beef
- 1 pound ground turkey
- 1/2 cup chopped onion
- 1 can (15-1/2 ounces) kidney beans, rinsed and drained
- 1 can (15-1/2 ounces) mild chili beans, undrained
- 1/2 cup chopped green pepper
- 4 teaspoons chili powder
- 1 teaspoon salt
- 1 teaspoon paprika
- 1 teaspoon cumin seed
- 1/2 teaspoon garlic salt
- 1/2 teaspoon dried oregano
- 1/4 teaspoon crushed red pepper flakes
- 3 cups V8 juice

DUMPLINGS:
- 1 cup mashed potato flakes
- 1 cup all-purpose flour
- 1 tablespoon minced fresh parsley
- 2 teaspoons baking powder
- 1/2 teaspoon salt
- 1 cup milk
- 1 egg, beaten

In a 5-qt. Dutch oven, cook beef, turkey and onion over medium heat until meat is no longer pink; drain. Add the next 11 ingredients; bring to a boil. Reduce heat; cover and simmer for 30 minutes, stirring occasionally.

In a medium bowl, combine the first five dumpling ingredients. Add milk and egg; stir just until moistened. Let rest for 3 minutes. Drop by tablespoonfuls into simmering chili. Cover and cook for 15 minutes. **Yield:** 8 servings (2 quarts).

inside-out brussels sprouts

Shirley Max, Cape Girardeau, Missouri
There were seven of us children when I was a girl, and I was the second oldest. I began cooking as soon as I could reach the stove and stir a pot. I'm a widow, so I usually make this for large gatherings. It's so quick and easy. The recipe was given to me when my husband and I were caring for foster children who enjoyed beef dishes.

- 1-1/2 cups uncooked instant rice
- 1 medium onion, chopped
- 2 eggs, lightly beaten
- 1-1/2 teaspoons garlic salt
- 1/2 teaspoon pepper
- 2 pounds ground beef
- 1 package (10 ounces) frozen brussels sprouts
- 2 cans (15 ounces *each*) tomato sauce
- 1 cup water
- 1 teaspoon dried thyme

In a large bowl, combine the first five ingredients; crumble beef over mixture and mix well. Cut an X in the core of each brussels sprout. Shape a scant 1/4 cupful around each frozen brussels sprout to form a meatball. Place in an ungreased 15-in. x 10-in. x 1-in. baking dish.

Combine tomato sauce, water and thyme; pour over meatballs. Cover and bake at 350° for 1 hour and 15 minutes or until meatballs are no longer pink. **Yield:** 8-10 servings.

beefy taco dip

Faye Parker, Bedford, Nova Scotia

This taco dip is actually a combination of several different recipes I received from friends. I just experimented till I came up with my favorite! It's always a hit when I carry it to family gatherings, church potlucks, etc.

- 1 package (8 ounces) cream cheese, softened
- 1 cup (8 ounces) sour cream
- 3/4 cup mayonnaise
- 1 pound ground beef
- 1 envelope taco seasoning mix
- 1 can (8 ounces) tomato sauce
- 2 cups (8 ounces) shredded cheddar *or* taco cheese
- 4 cups shredded lettuce
- 2 medium tomatoes, diced
- 1 small onion, diced
- 1 medium green pepper, diced

Tortilla chips

In a small mixing bowl, beat the cream cheese, sour cream and mayonnaise until smooth. Spread on a 12- to 14-in. pizza pan or serving dish. Refrigerate for 1 hour.

In a saucepan over medium heat, cook beef until no longer pink; drain. Add taco seasoning and tomato sauce; cook and stir for 5 minutes. Cool completely. Spread over cream cheese layer. Refrigerate. Just before serving, sprinkle with cheese, lettuce, tomatoes, onion and green pepper. Serve with chips. **Yield:** 16-20 servings.

beef and sauerkraut dinner

Marilyn Dietz, White, South Dakota

I've been making this one-dish meal for more than 30 years. The original recipe called for a single can of sauerkraut—but that wasn't enough for us! My husband is pastor to two small-town congregations. Among other occasions, I enjoy preparing this for church potlucks.

- 1 egg, lightly beaten
- 1-1/2 cups soft rye bread crumbs
- 1/3 cup milk
- 1/4 cup chopped onion
- 1 tablespoon cider vinegar
- 1-1/2 teaspoons caraway seed
- 1 teaspoon salt
- 1-1/2 pounds ground beef
- 1 tablespoon vegetable oil
- 2 cans (15 ounces *each*) sliced potatoes, drained
- 2 cans (14 ounces *each*) sauerkraut, undrained
- 2 tablespoons minced fresh parsley
- 1/4 cup *each* mayonnaise and horseradish, optional

In a bowl, combine the first seven ingredients; crumble beef over mixture and mix well. Shape into 1-1/2-in. balls. In a Dutch oven over medium heat, brown meatballs in oil; drain.

Add potatoes and sauerkraut; mix well. Bring to a boil. Reduce heat; cover and simmer for 15-20 minutes or until meatballs are no longer pink. Sprinkle with parsley. If sauce is desired, combine mayonnaise and horseradish; serve on the side. **Yield:** 6-8 servings.

pasta meatball stew

Pat Jelinek, Kitchener, Ontario

Growing up on the farm, I participated in 4-H cooking club activities. Nowadays, I like to visit Mom, Dad and their varied animals…including a llama.

- 1 egg, lightly beaten
- 1/4 cup dry bread crumbs
- 1/4 cup milk
- 1/2 teaspoon ground mustard
- 1/2 teaspoon salt
- 1/2 teaspoon pepper
- 1 pound ground beef
- 1 tablespoon vegetable oil

SAUCE:

- 1 cup chopped onion
- 2 garlic cloves, minced
- 1 tablespoon vegetable oil
- 2 tablespoons all-purpose flour
- 1-1/2 cups beef broth
- 1 can (14-1/2 ounces) diced tomatoes, undrained
- 2 tablespoons tomato paste
- 1 bay leaf
- 3/4 teaspoon dried thyme
- 1/2 teaspoon salt
- 1-1/2 cups sliced carrots
- 1-1/2 cups chopped zucchini
- 1 cup chopped green pepper
- 1 cup chopped sweet red pepper
- 1 tablespoon minced fresh parsley
- 2 cups cooked pasta

Combine first six ingredients; crumble beef over mixture and mix well. Shape into 1-in. balls. In a Dutch oven over medium heat, brown meatballs in oil; drain and set aside.

In same pan, saute onion and garlic in oil until onion is tender. Blend in flour. Gradually add broth, stirring constantly; bring to a boil. Cook and stir 1-2 minutes or until thickened. Add tomatoes, paste, bay leaf, thyme and salt; mix well. Add meatballs and carrots; bring to a boil. Reduce heat; cover and simmer 30 minutes. Add zucchini and peppers; bring to a boil. Reduce heat; cover and simmer 10-15 minutes or until vegetables are tender and meatballs are no longer pink. Add parsley and pasta; heat through. Remove bay leaf. **Yield:** 6-8 servings.

prize winning tips

★Save both time and money by buying ground beef in large quantity and cooking it. Freeze serving-size portions in airtight containers for use in a variety of recipes during the months ahead.

Kathy Beliveau, Middletown, Connecticut

★When shaping meatballs, be careful not to overmix or they will become very firm and tough.

Joy Rackham, Chimacum, Washington

ground beef turnovers

Wendy Tomlinson, Echo Bay, Ontario

My husband likes these turnovers so much that he even eats them cold!

    4 cups all-purpose flour
    1 tablespoon sugar
    2 teaspoons salt
1-3/4 cups shortening
  1/2 cup ice water
    1 egg, lightly beaten
    1 tablespoon vinegar
FILLING:
    2 pounds uncooked ground beef
    1 cup diced carrots
    2 medium potatoes, peeled and cut
      into 1/4-inch cubes
    1 medium onion, chopped
    1 to 2 teaspoons salt
  1/4 teaspoon pepper
Half-and-half cream

In a bowl, combine flour, sugar and salt; cut in shortening until mixture resembles coarse crumbs. Combine the water, egg and vinegar; mix well. Add to shortening mixture, 1 tablespoon at a time, tossing lightly with a fork until mixture forms a ball. Cover and chill for 30 minutes. Meanwhile, combine the first six filling ingredients.

Divide pastry into 15 equal portions. On a lightly floured surface, roll out one portion into a 6-1/2-in. circle. Mound a heaping 1/3 cup filling on half of circle. Moisten edges with water; fold dough over filling and press edges with a fork to seal. Transfer to a greased baking sheet. Repeat with remaining pastry and filling.

Cut three slits in top of each turnover; brush with cream. Bake at 375° for 35-40 minutes or until vegetables are tender and crust is golden. **Yield:** 15 turnovers.

sloppy joe pie

Kathy McCreary, Goddard, Kansas

To be honest, I don't hear many compliments on this dish…folks are always too busy eating! I developed the recipe by grabbing ingredients from my refrigerator and cupboards one "crunch time" when I needed an easy dish.

    1 pound ground beef
  1/2 cup chopped onion
    1 can (8 ounces) tomato sauce
    1 can (8-3/4 ounces) whole kernel corn, drained
  1/4 cup water
    1 envelope sloppy joe seasoning mix
    1 can (10 ounces) refrigerated biscuits
    2 tablespoons milk
  1/3 cup cornmeal
    1 cup (8 ounces) shredded cheddar cheese,
      divided

In a skillet, cook beef with onion until meat is no longer pink; drain. Stir in the tomato sauce, corn, water and sloppy joe seasoning; cook over medium heat until bubbly. Reduce heat and simmer for 5 minutes; remove from the heat and set aside.

Separate biscuits and roll or flatten each to a 3-1/2-in. circle; dip both sides into milk and then into the cornmeal. Place seven biscuits around the sides and three on the bottom of an ungreased 9-in. pie plate. Press biscuits together to form a crust, leaving a scalloped edge around rim. Sprinkle with 1/2 cup cheese. Spoon meat mixture over cheese.

Bake at 375° for 20-25 minutes or until crust is deep golden brown. Sprinkle with remaining cheese. Let stand for 5 minutes before serving. **Yield:** 7 servings.

cajun burgers

Julie Culbertson, Bensalem, Pennsylvania
I found the original recipe for these burgers in a cookbook, then added and subtracted ingredients until they suited our taste.

CAJUN SEASONING BLEND:
- 3 tablespoons ground cumin
- 3 tablespoons dried oregano
- 1 tablespoon garlic powder
- 1 tablespoon paprika
- 2 teaspoons salt
- 1 teaspoon cayenne pepper

BURGERS:
- 1/4 cup finely chopped onion
- 1 teaspoon salt
- 1 teaspoon Cajun Seasoning Blend (recipe above)
- 1/2 to 1 teaspoon hot pepper sauce
- 1/2 teaspoon dried thyme
- 1/4 teaspoon dried basil
- 1 garlic clove, minced
- 1 pound ground beef
- 4 hamburger buns

Sauteed onions, optional

Combine all seasoning blend ingredients in a small bowl or resealable plastic bag; mix well. In a bowl, combine the first seven burger ingredients; crumble beef over mixture and mix well. Shape into four patties.

Cook in a skillet or grill over medium-hot heat for 4-5 minutes per side or until burgers reach desired doneness. Serve on buns; top with sauteed onions if desired. Store remaining seasoning blend in an airtight container. **Yield:** 4 servings.

all-purpose meat sauce

Sonja Fontaine, Winnipeg, Manitoba
Experimenting with different herbs and spices led to this sauce…my husband does not like bland food! I now make it for him and our three children at least once a week.

- 1 pound ground beef
- 1 to 2 garlic cloves, minced
- 1 can (15 ounces) tomato sauce
- 1 can (10-3/4 ounces) tomato soup, undiluted
- 1/4 cup grated Parmesan cheese
- 1 tablespoon Worcestershire sauce
- 1-1/2 teaspoons dried oregano
- 1 teaspoon dried basil
- 1/2 teaspoon sugar
- 1/2 teaspoon salt
- 1/2 teaspoon dried parsley flakes
- 1/4 teaspoon crushed red pepper flakes

Pinch *each* dried thyme, tarragon and ground cinnamon

Hot pepper sauce and cayenne pepper to taste

In a large skillet or Dutch oven, cook the beef and garlic until meat is no longer pink; drain. Stir in remaining ingredients. Simmer, uncovered, for 30 minutes or until sauce is as thick as desired, stirring occasionally.

Serve over pasta or rice, or use for making lasagna, pizza, chili dogs, tacos or sloppy joes. **Yield:** 4 cups.

PICK OF THE PORK

#1

FARMHOUSE PORK
AND APPLE PIE

farmhouse pork and apple pie
GRAND PRIZE WINNER

Practical, palate-pleasing pork is the choice of many cooks for a hearty main dish. It's such a popular meat because it goes well with a wide variety of flavors and cooks up tender and juicy. And pork is so versatile it can be served often without boring the taste buds.

> "I've always loved pork and apples together, and this recipe combines them nicely..."

Nothing proves that point better than our Pick of the Pork contest. Great cooks from across the country entered over 2,500 recipes in all, featuring ribs, chops, roasts, tenderloins and more. Our judges had the difficult but delicious job of selecting the winners. Farmhouse Pork and Apple Pie won the Grand Prize.

"I've always loved pork and apples together, and this recipe combines them nicely to create a comforting main dish," says Suzanne Strocsher of Bothell, Washington. "It calls for a bit of preparation, but my family and I agree that its wonderful flavor makes it well worth the extra effort."

1 pound sliced bacon, cut into 2-inch pieces
3 medium onions, chopped
3 pounds boneless pork, cubed
3/4 cup all-purpose flour
Vegetable oil, optional
3 tart cooking apples, peeled and chopped
1 teaspoon rubbed sage
1/2 teaspoon ground nutmeg
1 teaspoon salt
1/4 teaspoon pepper
1 cup apple cider
1/2 cup water
4 medium potatoes, peeled and cubed
1/2 cup milk
5 tablespoons butter, *divided*
Additional salt and pepper
Snipped fresh parsley, optional

Cook bacon in an ovenproof 12-in. skillet until crisp. Remove with a slotted spoon to paper towels to drain. In drippings, saute onions until tender; remove with a slotted spoon and set aside.

Dust pork lightly with flour. Brown a third at a time in drippings, adding oil if needed. Remove from the heat and drain. To pork, add bacon, onions, apples, sage, nutmeg, salt and pepper. Stir in apple cider and water. Cover and bake at 325° for 2 hours or until the pork is tender.

In a saucepan, cook potatoes in boiling water until tender. Drain and mash with milk and 3 tablespoons butter. Add salt and pepper to taste. Remove skillet from the oven and spread potatoes over pork mixture. Melt remaining butter; brush over potatoes.

Broil 6 in. from the heat for 5 minutes or until topping is browned. Sprinkle with parsley if desired. **Yield:** 10 servings.

tangy barbecued spareribs

Bette Brotzel, Billings, Montana

My husband is a meat cutter at a supermarket and likes to find new ways to smoke or barbecue meat. Several years ago, he discovered this recipe for pork ribs covered in a rich tangy sauce. It was an instant success with our family and friends.

- 4 pounds pork spareribs, cut into serving-size pieces
- 1 medium onion, quartered
- 2 teaspoons salt
- 1/4 teaspoon pepper

SAUCE:
- 1/2 cup cider vinegar
- 1/2 cup packed brown sugar
- 1/2 cup ketchup
- 1/4 cup chili sauce
- 1/4 cup Worcestershire sauce
- 2 tablespoons chopped onion
- 1 tablespoon lemon juice
- 1/2 teaspoon ground mustard
- 1 garlic clove, minced

Dash cayenne pepper

In a large kettle or Dutch oven, place ribs and onion; sprinkle with salt and pepper. Add enough water to cover ribs; bring to a boil. Reduce heat; cover and simmer for 1-1/2 hours or until tender; drain.

Combine all of the sauce ingredients in a saucepan. Simmer, uncovered, for 1 hour or until slightly thickened, stirring occasionally. Arrange the ribs on a rack in a broiler pan. Brush with sauce. Broil 5 in. from the heat for 5 minutes on each side, brushing frequently with sauce. **Yield:** 4 servings.

southwestern pork salad

Sue Cunningham, Prospect, Ohio

As pork producers, we're proud to cook and serve the delicious product we raise. This salad is refreshing and colorful. It's a succulent showcase for pork. I know your family will enjoy it as much as we do.

- 2 cups cooked pork strips
- 1 can (16 ounces) kidney beans, rinsed and drained
- 1/2 cup sliced ripe olives
- 1 medium onion, chopped
- 1 large green pepper, chopped
- 1 large tomato, chopped
- 2 tablespoons sugar
- 1/4 cup cider vinegar
- 1/4 cup vegetable oil
- 1 teaspoon ground mustard
- 1 teaspoon ground cumin
- 1 teaspoon dried oregano
- 1/2 teaspoon salt
- 2 tablespoons minced fresh parsley

In a large bowl, toss pork, beans, olives, onion, green pepper and tomato. Combine remaining ingredients in a jar with tight-fitting lid; shake well.

Pour over the pork mixture and toss gently. Cover and refrigerate for 4-6 hours, stirring occasionally. **Yield:** 4 servings.

pork chops ole

Laura Turner, Channelview, Texas

This recipe is a fun and simple way to give pork chops south-of-the-border flair. The flavorful seasoning, rice and melted cheddar cheese make this dish a crowd-pleaser. A dear friend shared this recipe with me several years ago.

  6 **loin pork chops (1/2 inch thick)**
  2 **tablespoons vegetable oil**
Seasoned salt and pepper to taste
  3/4 **cup uncooked long grain rice**
1-1/2 **cups water**
  1 **can (8 ounces) tomato sauce**
  2 **tablespoons taco seasoning mix**
  1 **medium green pepper, chopped**
  1/2 **cup shredded cheddar cheese**

In a large skillet, brown pork chops in oil; sprinkle with seasoned salt and pepper. Meanwhile, in a greased 13-in. x 9-in. x 2-in. baking dish, combine rice, water, tomato sauce and taco seasoning; mix well. Arrange chops over rice; top with green pepper.

Cover and bake at 350° for 1-1/2 hours. Uncover and sprinkle with cheese; return to oven until cheese is melted. **Yield:** 4-6 servings.

---

*When baking a pork chop casserole, keep it covered for the first 45 minutes. Uncover toward the end of baking time to allow a little browning.

Mardel Stenzel, Wells, Minnesota

---

roast pork with apple topping

Virginia Barrett, Rochester, New York

I enjoy cooking and am constantly on the lookout for new recipes to try. I feel very fortunate when I find a dish like this that becomes a family favorite. Ever since I found this recipe several years ago, it's the main way I fix pork loin.

  2 **tablespoons all-purpose flour**
1-3/4 **teaspoons salt, *divided***
  1 **teaspoon ground mustard**
  1 **teaspoon caraway seed**
  1/2 **teaspoon sugar**
  1/4 **teaspoon pepper**
  1/4 **teaspoon rubbed sage**
  1 **pork loin roast (4 to 5 pounds)**
1-1/2 **cups applesauce**
  1/2 **cup packed brown sugar**
  1/4 **teaspoon ground mace**

In a small bowl, combine flour, 1-1/2 teaspoons salt, mustard, caraway, sugar, pepper and sage; rub over roast. Cover and let stand for 30 minutes. Place on a greased baking rack, fat side up, in a roasting pan. Bake, uncovered, at 325° for 1 hour.

Combine applesauce, brown sugar, mace and remaining salt; mix well. Spread over roast. Roast 1 hour longer or until the internal temperature reaches 160°-170°. Let stand 15 minutes before slicing. **Yield:** 8-10 servings.

sweet-and-sour pork

Cherry Williams, St. Albert, Alberta

After my sister moved away to the university, I used to visit her on weekends. She often made this wonderful and tangy pork dish. Now, every time I make it for my family, it reminds me of those special visits.

- 1 **pound pork tenderloin**
- 2 **cans (8 ounces *each*) pineapple tidbits**
- 1/3 **cup ketchup**
- 1/3 **cup water**
- 2 **tablespoons *each* soy sauce, vinegar, brown sugar and cornstarch**
- 3/4 **teaspoon salt**
- 1/4 **teaspoon pepper**
- 1/4 **teaspoon ground ginger**
- 2 **tablespoons vegetable oil**
- 1 **medium onion, chopped**
- 1 **green pepper, cut into thin strips**

Hot cooked rice

Cut the tenderloin into 1-1/2-in. x 1/4-in. strips; set aside. Drain pineapple, reserving juice in a small bowl. Set pineapple aside. To juice, add ketchup, water, soy sauce, vinegar, brown sugar, cornstarch, salt, pepper and ginger; stir until smooth.

Heat oil in a large skillet or wok on high; stir-fry pork and onion for 5-7 minutes or until pork is no longer pink. Stir pineapple juice mixture; add to skillet. Cook and stir until thickened and bubbly. Add pineapple and green pepper. Reduce heat; cover and cook for 5 minutes. Serve immediately over rice. **Yield:** 4 servings.

spicy pork chili

Christine Hartry, Emo, Ontario

This zippy chili is a pleasant change from the traditional beef chili recipes I've tried. It tastes so good served with your garden-fresh steamed green beans, sliced cucumbers and hot crusty bread. It's satisfying on a cold day.

- 1 **pound ground pork**
- 2 **large onions, chopped**
- 4 **garlic cloves, minced**
- 1 **medium sweet red pepper, chopped**
- 1 **medium green pepper, chopped**
- 1 **cup chopped celery**
- 2 **cans (14-1/2 ounces *each*) diced tomatoes, undrained**
- 1 **can (16 ounces) kidney beans, rinsed and drained**
- 1 **can (6 ounces) tomato paste**
- 3/4 **cup water**
- 2 **teaspoons brown sugar**
- 1 **teaspoon dried oregano**
- 1 **teaspoon chili powder**
- 1/4 **teaspoon dried red pepper flakes**
- 1/4 **teaspoon cayenne pepper**

Dash hot pepper sauce

In a Dutch oven, cook pork and onions until pork is no longer pink; drain. Stir in the garlic, peppers and celery; cook for 5 minutes. Add remaining ingredients; bring to a boil. Reduce heat; cover and simmer for 45 minutes. **Yield:** 6-8 servings (2-1/2 quarts).

pork with mustard sauce

Irma Pomeroy, Enfield, Connecticut

Back when I was a young girl, I couldn't wait until I was grown up and could start cooking for my own family! Now that I am, I really enjoy using pork in a variety of dishes. The tender meat and the rich mustard sauce in this recipe are simply delectable together.

- **1 pound pork tenderloin**
- **2 tablespoons butter**
- **1/2 cup beef broth**
- **3/4 teaspoon dried tarragon**
- **1/2 cup heavy whipping cream**
- **1 tablespoon Dijon mustard**
- **Salt and pepper to taste**
- **Hot cooked noodles, optional**

Cut the pork tenderloin into eight pieces. Slice each piece of pork again, but do not cut all of the way through; open and flatten each piece, pounding slightly with meat mallet.

In a large skillet over medium-high heat, cook the pork in butter until no longer pink, about 5-6 minutes per side. Remove to a serving dish and keep warm; discard the drippings.

In the same skillet, cook broth and tarragon over high heat until reduced by half. Reduce heat; stir in whipping cream and mustard. Season with salt and pepper. Spoon over the pork. Serve with noodles if desired. **Yield:** 4 servings.

---

prize winning tips

* * * * *

*Leftover pork chops make wonderful sandwiches. Just remove meat from the bones and chop in a food processor. Reheat the meat and serve on buns.

Deborah Imioli-Schriver, Amherst, New York

*If you're preparing a pork dish in a slow cooker, add fresh herbs at the end of the cooking time for pleasing taste and pretty color.

Elizabeth Mullett, Haverhill, Massachusetts

*Here's an easy marinade for grilled pork chops: for 4 chops, combine 1/2 cup each soy sauce, water and honey. Pour over chops and marinate, covered, in the refrigerator overnight. Drain and discard marinade and grill the pork chops.

Rhea Lease, Colman, South Dakota

*If you want succulent chops, choose those that are about 1 inch thick. Thin pork chops have a tendency to dry out no matter how careful you are.

Elaine Williams, Sebastopol, California

---

runners-up

pork chow mein

Helen Carpenter, Marble Falls, Texas
I give all the credit for my love of cooking and baking to my mother, grandmother and mother-in-law. That trio inspired delicious dishes like this hearty skillet dinner. When we get a taste for stir-fry, this dish hits the spot.

- 1 pound boneless pork loin
- 2 garlic cloves, minced
- 4 tablespoons soy sauce, *divided*
- 1 cup chicken broth
- 2 tablespoons cornstarch
- 1/2 to 1 teaspoon ground ginger
- 1 tablespoon vegetable oil
- 1 cup thinly sliced carrots
- 1 cup thinly sliced celery
- 1 cup chopped onion
- 1 cup coarsely chopped cabbage
- 1 cup coarsely chopped fresh spinach

Hot cooked rice, optional

Cut pork into 4-in. x 1/2-in. x 1/4-in. strips; place in a bowl. Add garlic and 2 tablespoons soy sauce. Cover and refrigerate 2-4 hours. Meanwhile, combine broth, cornstarch, ginger and remaining soy sauce; mix well and set aside.

Heat oil in a large skillet or wok on high; stir-fry pork until no longer pink. Remove and keep warm. Add carrots and celery; stir-fry 3-4 minutes. Add onion, cabbage and spinach; stir-fry 2-3 minutes. Stir broth mixture and add to skillet along with pork. Cook and stir until broth thickens, about 3-4 minutes. Serve immediately over rice if desired. **Yield:** 6 servings.

pork tenderloin diane

Janie Thorpe, Tullahoma, Tennessee
We have pork at least once a week, and this is one dish we especially enjoy. Moist tender pork "medallions" are served up in a savory sauce for a combination that's irresistible. I'm not sure where the recipe came from, but I'm glad I have it.

- 1 pork tenderloin (about 1 pound)
- 1 tablespoon lemon-pepper seasoning
- 2 tablespoons butter
- 2 tablespoons lemon juice
- 1 tablespoon Worcestershire sauce
- 1 teaspoon Dijon mustard
- 1 tablespoon minced fresh parsley

Cut tenderloin into eight pieces; place each piece between two pieces of plastic wrap or waxed paper and flatten to 1/2-in. thickness. Sprinkle with lemon-pepper seasoning.

Melt butter in a large skillet over medium heat; cook pork for 3-4 minutes on each side or until no longer pink and juices run clear. Remove to a serving platter and keep warm.

To the pan juices, add lemon juice, Worcestershire sauce and mustard; heat through, stirring occasionally. Pour over the pork and sprinkle with parsley. Serve immediately. **Yield:** 4 servings.

old-world stuffed pork chops

Jeanne Schuyler, Wauwatosa, Wisconsin
Years ago, a relative ran a restaurant in downtown Milwaukee, where several well-known German restaurants still operate. This is one of the recipes she developed. The savory stuffing and juicy pork chops are always a hit.

   4 pork chops (1/2 inch thick)
   1 to 2 tablespoons vegetable oil
Salt and pepper to taste
   3 cups dry unseasoned bread cubes
   1 can (16 ounces) cream-style corn
   1 egg, lightly beaten
   1 teaspoon grated onion
   1/2 teaspoon rubbed sage
   1/2 teaspoon dried basil
   1/2 teaspoon salt
   1/4 teaspoon pepper

In a skillet, brown pork chops in oil on both sides; sprinkle with salt and pepper. Meanwhile, in a bowl, combine remaining ingredients and mix well. Alternate the pork chops and stuffing lengthwise in a greased 3-qt. or 11-in. x 7-in. x 2-in. baking dish. Bake, uncovered, at 350° for 1 hour. **Yield:** 4 servings.

> *To make pork roast even tastier, top it with a jar of all-fruit apricot preserves. Pour 1/2 cup apple juice over all and sprinkle with lemon-pepper seasoning.
> Bettyrae Easley, Anchorage, Alaska

tuscan pork roast

Elinor Stabile, Canmore, Alberta
Everyone's eager to eat after the wonderful aroma of this well-seasoned pork roast baking in the oven tempts us all afternoon. This is a great Sunday dinner with little fuss to prepare. Since I found this recipe a few years ago, it's become a favorite with our seven grown children and their families.

   5 to 8 garlic cloves, peeled
   1 tablespoon dried rosemary
   1 tablespoon olive oil
   1/2 teaspoon salt
   1 boneless pork loin roast (3 to 4 pounds)

In a blender or food processor, combine the garlic, rosemary, olive oil and salt; blend until the mixture turns to paste. Rub over the roast; cover and let stand for 30 minutes.

   Place on a greased baking rack, fat side up, in a roasting pan. Bake, uncovered, at 325° for 2 to 2-1/2 hours or until the internal temperature reaches 160°-170°. Let the roast stand for 15 minutes before slicing. **Yield:** 10-12 servings.

BEEFING IT UP
#1

TANGY BEEF BRISKET

tangy beef brisket

Chances are when you plan a meal, you first think of meat, and none whets a country appetite more than beef. So it's no surprise the "steaks" were high in our Beefing It Up contest...and so were the roasts, ribs, tenderloins and briskets.

> "The meat is so juicy and tender, everyone requests seconds."

Whether roasted, broiled, pan-fried, slow-cooked or barbecued, all had our testers raving for days over their "must-eat" juicy, fork-tender taste.

From hundreds of prime possibilities, our judges narrowed the field to a few choice dishes. Finally, they concurred on a cut-above entree—Tangy Beef Brisket was chosen as the Grand Prize Winner.

"The secret's in the sauce," says Jacque Watkins from Green River, Wyoming. "The sweetness of brown sugar and bite of horseradish don't disguise the flavor of the meat—in fact, they enhance it. The meat is so juicy and tender, everyone requests seconds."

1 large onion, diced
1/2 cup butter
1 bottle (28 ounces) ketchup
1-1/2 cups packed brown sugar
1/2 cup Worcestershire sauce
1/3 cup lemon juice
2 tablespoons chili powder
1-1/2 teaspoons hot pepper sauce
1 teaspoon prepared horseradish
1 teaspoon salt
1/2 teaspoon garlic powder
1 boneless beef brisket (6 pounds)

In a saucepan, saute onion in butter until tender. Add the next nine ingredients; bring to a boil. Reduce heat; simmer, uncovered, for 30-40 minutes.

Place brisket in a roasting pan. Add 3 cups of sauce. Cover and bake at 350° for 4 hours, basting occasionally. Skim fat. Remove brisket; thinly slice the beef and return to pan. Add remaining sauce if desired. **Yield:** 12-14 servings (6 cups sauce).

Editor's Note: This is a fresh beef brisket, not corned beef.

old-fashioned pot roast

Georgia Edgington, Crystal, Minnesota

Every time I fix this recipe for friends, it's asked for—and usually by the husbands! As a mom who works full time, I also like how easy it is to prepare. It's one of our favorites. Some people I've shared the recipe with have used a beef brisket in place of the regular roast. For a bit different taste, I at times add red wine vinegar. My mom started me cooking young. I made my first from-scratch Thanksgiving dinner at age 13. After that, I figured I could tackle just about any cooking!

  1 **eye of round roast (3 to 4 pounds)**
  1 **bottle (12 ounces) chili sauce**
  1 **cup water**
  1 **envelope onion soup mix**
  4 **medium potatoes, cut into 1-inch pieces**
  5 **medium carrots, cut into 1-inch pieces**
  2 **celery ribs, cut into 1-inch pieces**

Place roast in an ungreased roasting pan. Combine the chili sauce, water and onion soup mix; pour over roast. Cover and bake at 350° for 2 hours.

  Cut roast into 1/2-in. slices; return to pan. Top with potatoes, carrots and celery. Cover and bake 1 hour longer or until vegetables are tender, stirring the vegetables once. **Yield:** 8 servings.

sesame steaks

Elaine Anderson, Aliquippa, Pennsylvania

There's enough flavor in these steaks to allow the side dish to be simple. So consider serving them with baked potatoes, rice pilaf or another plain vegetable and salad. The meal has always gone over big when I've fixed it for my husband and friends helping out with his latest home construction project.

1/2 **cup soy sauce**
  2 **tablespoons brown sugar**
  2 **tablespoons vegetable oil**
  2 **tablespoons sesame seeds**
  2 **teaspoons onion powder**
  2 **teaspoons lemon juice**
1/4 **teaspoon ground ginger**
  4 **T-bone steaks (about 1 inch thick)**

In a large resealable plastic bag or shallow glass container, combine the first seven ingredients; mix well. Add steaks and turn to coat. Cover and refrigerate for at least 4 hours.

  Drain and discard marinade. Grill steaks, uncovered, over medium heat for 5-7 minutes on each side or until meat reaches desired doneness (for rare, a meat thermometer should read 140°; medium, 160°; well-done, 170°). **Yield:** 4 servings.

herb-crusted roast beef

Teri Lindquist, Gurnee, Illinois

It's more than 20 years now I've been married to a man who loves beef. For a long time, though, I was reluctant to cook a roast for fear of ruining it. Finally, I started buying roasts on sale and experimenting. This recipe was the fabulous result.

> 1 boneless rump roast (4-1/2 to 5 pounds)
> 2 garlic cloves, minced
> 2 tablespoons Dijon mustard
> 2 tablespoons lemon juice
> 2 tablespoons olive oil
> 2 tablespoons Worcestershire sauce
> 1 tablespoon dried parsley flakes
> 1 teaspoon dried basil
> 1 teaspoon salt
> 1 teaspoon coarsely ground pepper
> 1/2 teaspoon dried tarragon
> 1/2 teaspoon dried thyme
> 2-1/3 cups water, *divided*
> 2 teaspoons beef bouillon granules
> 1/4 to 1/3 cup all-purpose flour

Place roast with fat side up in an ungreased roasting pan. Combine the next five ingredients; pour over roast. Combine parsley, basil, salt, pepper, tarragon and thyme; rub over roast. Bake, uncovered, at 325° for 1-3/4 to 2-1/4 hours or until meat reaches desired doneness (for rare, a meat thermometer should read 140°; medium, 160°; well-done, 170°). Remove to a warm serving platter. Let stand for 10-15 minutes.

Meanwhile, add 2 cups water and bouillon to pan drippings; bring to a boil. Combine flour and remaining water until smooth; gradually add to pan. Cook and stir until bubbly and thickened. Slice roast; serve with gravy. **Yield:** 10-12 servings.

chicken-fried cube steaks

Toni Holcomb, Rogersville, Missouri

Here in the Ozarks, country-fried steak is a staple. These are wonderful served with mashed potatoes and some freshly baked rolls. I developed the recipe to meet the spicy tastes of my family.

> 2-1/2 cups all-purpose flour, *divided*
> 2 tablespoons black pepper
> 1 to 2 tablespoons white pepper
> 2 tablespoons garlic powder
> 1 tablespoon paprika
> 1-1/2 teaspoons salt
> 1 teaspoon ground cumin
> 1/4 to 1/2 teaspoon cayenne pepper
> 2 cups buttermilk
> 2 cans (12 ounces *each*) evaporated milk
> 8 cube steaks (4 ounces *each*)
> Oil for frying
> 1 teaspoon Worcestershire sauce
> Dash hot pepper sauce

In a shallow bowl, combine 2 cups flour and seasonings; set aside. In another bowl, combine buttermilk and evaporated milk. Remove 3-1/2 cups for gravy and set aside. Dip cube steaks into buttermilk mixture, then into flour mixture, coating well. Repeat.

In a skillet, heat 1/2 in. of oil on high. Fry steaks, a few at a time, for 5-7 minutes. Turn carefully and cook 5 minutes longer or until coating is crisp and meat is no longer pink. Remove steaks and keep warm.

Drain, reserving 1/3 cup drippings in the skillet; stir remaining flour into drippings until smooth. Cook and stir over medium heat for 5 minutes or until golden brown. Whisk in reserved buttermilk mixture; bring to a boil. Cook and stir for 2 minutes. Add Worcestershire sauce and hot pepper sauce. Serve with steaks. **Yield:** 8 servings (4 cups gravy).

sour cream swiss steak

Barb Benting, Grand Rapids, Michigan

One year, after we'd purchased half a beef from a local cattle raiser, I went on a full-scale search for new and different recipes. This is one I found—my family loved it from the very first bite. I've shared it with friends at work, too (I'm a waitress). They agree it's a nice change from regular Swiss steak.

- 1/3 cup all-purpose flour
- 1-1/2 teaspoons *each* salt, pepper, paprika and ground mustard
- 3 pounds boneless round steak, cut into serving-size pieces
- 3 tablespoons vegetable oil
- 3 tablespoons butter
- 1-1/2 cups water
- 1-1/2 cups (12 ounces) sour cream
- 1 cup finely chopped onion
- 2 garlic cloves, minced
- 1/3 cup soy sauce
- 1/4 to 1/3 cup packed brown sugar
- 3 tablespoons all-purpose flour

Additional paprika, optional

In a shallow bowl, combine flour, salt, pepper, paprika and mustard; dredge the steak. In a large skillet, heat oil and butter. Cook steak on both sides until browned. Carefully add water; cover and simmer for 30 minutes.

In a bowl, combine the sour cream, onion, garlic, soy sauce, brown sugar and flour; stir until smooth. Transfer steak to a greased 2-1/2-qt. baking dish; add sour cream mixture. Cover and bake at 325° for 1-1/2 hours or until tender. Sprinkle with paprika if desired. **Yield:** 6-8 servings.

stew with confetti dumplings

Lucile Cline, Wichita, Kansas

If you want a stew that will warm you to the bone, try this. My family particularly likes the dumplings.

- 2 pounds boneless chuck roast, cut into cubes
- 2 tablespoons vegetable oil
- 1/2 pound fresh mushrooms, halved
- 1 large onion, thinly sliced
- 1 garlic clove, minced
- 2 cans (14-1/2 ounces *each*) beef broth
- 1 teaspoon *each* salt and Italian seasoning
- 1/4 teaspoon pepper
- 1 bay leaf
- 1/3 cup all-purpose flour
- 1/2 cup water
- 1 package (10 ounces) frozen peas

DUMPLINGS:
- 1-1/2 cups biscuit/baking mix
- 2 tablespoons diced pimientos, drained
- 1 tablespoon minced chives
- 1/2 cup milk

In a Dutch oven, brown meat in oil. Add mushrooms, onion and garlic; cook until onion is tender, stirring occasionally. Stir in broth, Italian seasoning, salt, pepper and bay leaf; bring to a boil. Cover and simmer for 1-1/2 hours. Discard bay leaf. Combine the flour and water until smooth; stir into stew. Bring to a boil; cook and stir for 1 minute. Reduce heat. Stir in peas.

For dumplings, combine biscuit mix, pimientos and chives in a bowl. Stir in enough milk to form a soft dough. Drop by tablespoonfuls onto the simmering stew. Cover and simmer for 10-12 minutes or until dumplings test done (do not lift lid while simmering). Serve immediately. **Yield:** 10-12 servings (about 3 quarts).

pasta salad with steak

Julie DeRuwe, Oakville, Washington

While there are quite a few ingredients in this recipe, it doesn't take too long to make—and cleanup afterward's a snap.

- 3/4 cup olive oil
- 2 tablespoons lemon juice
- 2 teaspoons dried oregano
- 1 tablespoon Dijon mustard
- 2 teaspoons red wine vinegar
- 1 teaspoon sugar
- 1/2 teaspoon salt
- 1/2 teaspoon pepper
- 3 cups cooked small shell pasta
- 1 sirloin steak (1 pound)

RUB:
- 1 tablespoon olive oil
- 3 garlic cloves, minced
- 2 teaspoons dried oregano
- 2 teaspoons pepper
- 1 teaspoon sugar

SALAD:
- 2/3 cup diced cucumber
- 1/2 cup crumbled feta cheese
- 1/4 cup sliced ripe olives
- 1/4 cup chopped red onion
- 1/4 cup minced fresh parsley
- 1 jar (2 ounces) diced pimientos, drained

Iceberg *or* romaine lettuce

Combine the first eight ingredients; set half of the dressing aside. Place pasta in a bowl; add remaining dressing. Toss to coat; cover and refrigerate.

Pierce steak with a fork. Combine rub ingredients; rub over steak. Cover and refrigerate for at least 15 minutes. Grill steak, uncovered, over medium heat for 9-10 minutes on each side or until meat reaches desired doneness (for rare, a meat thermometer should read 140°; medium, 160°; well-done, 170°). Let stand 10 minutes.

Meanwhile, add cucumber, cheese, olives, onion, parsley and pimientos to pasta; mix well. Spoon onto a lettuce-lined platter. Slice steak and arrange over salad. Serve with reserved dressing. **Yield:** 4 servings.

---

prize winning tips

* One way to tenderize flank steak is to score it. Make shallow crisscrossed diamond-shaped cuts on both sides of the meat before cooking it.

Margaret Herz, Hastings, Nebraska

* I often use a steak pinwheel recipe when I'm unsure about the number of dinner guests to expect. You can feed as few or as many as you like simply by adjusting the number you prepare.

Ellen Baird, Kennewick, Washington

* A can of carbonated cola will tenderize and add flavor to pot roast.

Pam Rush, Salina, Kansas

runners-up

savory beef sandwiches

Lynn Williamson, Hayward, Wisconsin
Before heading to work in the morning, I'll get this going in the slow cooker. Then it's all ready to serve, usually with hard rolls and potato salad or another salad, as soon as my husband and I walk in. When my son—one of three children—moved to another state recently, I cut up beef roast in smaller portions, repackaged it and sent seasonings for a two-person slow cooker as his housewarming present.

- 1 tablespoon dried minced onion
- 2 teaspoons salt
- 2 teaspoons garlic powder
- 2 teaspoons dried oregano
- 1 teaspoon dried rosemary, crushed
- 1 teaspoon caraway seeds
- 1 teaspoon dried marjoram
- 1 teaspoon celery seed
- 1/4 teaspoon cayenne pepper
- 1 boneless chuck roast (3 to 4 pounds), halved
- 8 to 10 sandwich rolls, split

Combine seasonings; rub over roast. Place in a slow cooker. Cover and cook on low for 6-8 hours or until meat is tender. Shred with a fork. Serve on rolls. **Yield:** 8-10 servings.

Editor's Note: No liquid is added to the slow cooker. The moisture comes from the roast.

tenderloin with creamy garlic sauce

Beth Taylor, Chapin, South Carolina
Served with green beans, garlic mashed potatoes and seven-layer salad, this is the main course at my family's annual Christmas gathering. Even those who aren't fond of meat comment on its tenderness and flavor. Likely, since garlic goes well with everything, the sauce would be good with pork or poultry besides.

- 1 jar (8 ounces) Dijon mustard, *divided*
- 10 garlic cloves, *divided*
- 2 tablespoons whole black peppercorns, coarsely crushed, *divided*
- 3 tablespoons vegetable oil, *divided*
- 1 beef tenderloin (4 to 5 pounds), halved
- 2 cups heavy whipping cream
- 1 cup (8 ounces) sour cream

In a blender, combine half of the mustard, eight garlic cloves and 1 tablespoon peppercorns. Cover; process 1 minute, scraping sides occasionally. Add 1 tablespoon oil; process until a paste forms. Spread over beef.

In a large skillet, heat the remaining oil over medium-high heat. Brown beef on all sides. Transfer to an ungreased 13-in. x 9-in. x 2-in. baking dish. Cover and bake at 375° for 40-50 minutes or until meat reaches desired doneness (for rare, a meat thermometer should read 140°; medium, 160°; well-done, 170°). Remove to a warm serving platter. Let stand for 10-15 minutes.

Meanwhile, mince remaining garlic. In a saucepan, combine garlic, whipping cream, sour cream and remaining mustard and peppercorns. Cook and stir over low heat until heated through. Slice beef; serve with the sauce. **Yield:** 12-15 servings.

barbecued short ribs

Cheryl Niemela, Cokato, Minnesota
People like the blending of many different flavors in this recipe. I consider it a very special one and generally fix it for company. It receives rave reviews. I'm sure the sauce would also taste good on pork chops or chicken.

- 5 pounds bone-in short ribs, trimmed
- 2 medium onions, finely chopped
- 2 garlic cloves, minced
- 2 tablespoons olive oil
- 1 can (14-1/2 ounces) diced tomatoes, undrained
- 1 cup chili sauce
- 1/3 cup soy sauce
- 1/3 cup honey
- 1/4 cup packed brown sugar
- 1/4 cup ketchup
- 2 teaspoons chili powder
- 1/2 teaspoon ground ginger
- 1/8 teaspoon cayenne pepper
- 1/8 teaspoon dried oregano
- 1/8 teaspoon Liquid Smoke, optional

Place ribs in a Dutch oven; add water to cover by 2 in. Bring to a boil. Reduce heat; simmer, uncovered, for 1-1/2 to 2 hours or until tender.

Meanwhile, in a saucepan, saute onions and garlic in oil until tender. Add remaining ingredients; bring to a boil. Reduce heat; simmer, uncovered, for 30 minutes, stirring occasionally.

Drain ribs. Arrange on a broiler pan and baste with barbecue sauce. Broil 4 to 5 in. from the heat for 5-10 minutes on each side or until sauce is bubbly. **Yield:** 6-8 servings.

tender beef and noodles

Nancy Peterson, Farmington, British Columbia
Because I often work outside with my husband on our cattle ranch, I appreciate convenient recipes like this. The main dish cooks by itself and is ready for us when we come in the house. If you like, substitute stew meat for the roast. Either way, it's a hearty everyday meal with a special tasty twist.

- 1 boneless chuck roast (2 to 2-1/2 pounds), cut into 1-inch cubes
- 2 large onions, chopped
- 3 tablespoons butter
- 1 can (8 ounces) tomato sauce
- 2 teaspoons sugar
- 2 teaspoons paprika
- 2 teaspoons Worcestershire sauce
- 1 to 2 teaspoons salt
- 1-1/2 teaspoons caraway seeds
- 1 teaspoon dill weed
- 1/4 teaspoon pepper
- 1/8 teaspoon garlic powder
- 1 cup (8 ounces) sour cream

Hot cooked noodles

In a large saucepan or Dutch oven, cook beef and onions in butter until the meat is browned. Add the next nine ingredients; bring to a boil. Reduce heat; cover and simmer for 1-3/4 to 2 hours or until meat is tender. Remove from the heat; stir in sour cream. Serve over noodles. **Yield:** 4-6 servings.

COMFORTING CASSEROLES
#1

CHICKEN AND
DUMPLING
CASSEROLE

chicken and dumpling casserole

A hearty casserole can take the chill out of a cold evening, lift spirits and warm hearts. The versatility and convenience of casseroles, along with their stick-to-your-ribs goodness, have made them a mainstay in family meals.

"**This savory** meal-in-one **is one of my husband's** favorites."

Our Comforting Casseroles contest stirred the interest of readers from coast to coast, resulting in a kitchen full of recipes—over 6,000 in all!

The casseroles our judges selected as the winners will surely make regular appearances on your table whenever a warm, filling meal is in order...especially Grand Prize Winner Chicken and Dumpling Casserole shared by Sue Mackey of Galesburg, Illinois.

"This savory meal-in-one is one of my husband's favorites," says Sue. "He loves the fluffy dumplings with plenty of gravy poured over them. The basil adds just the right touch of flavor and makes the whole house smell so good while this dish cooks."

1/2 cup chopped onion
1/2 cup chopped celery
2 garlic cloves, minced
1/4 cup butter
1/2 cup all-purpose flour
2 teaspoons sugar
1 teaspoon salt
1 teaspoon dried basil
1/2 teaspoon pepper
4 cups chicken broth
1 package (10 ounces) frozen green peas
4 cups cubed cooked chicken

DUMPLINGS:
2 cups biscuit/baking mix
2 teaspoons dried basil
2/3 cup milk

In a large saucepan, saute onion, celery and garlic in butter until tender. Add flour, sugar, salt, basil, pepper and broth; bring to a boil. Cook and stir for 1 minute; reduce heat. Add peas and cook for 5 minutes, stirring constantly. Stir in chicken. Pour into a greased 13-in. x 9-in. x 2-in. baking dish.

For dumplings, combine biscuit mix and basil in a bowl. Stir in milk with a fork until moistened. Drop by tablespoonfuls onto casserole (12 dumplings).

Bake, uncovered, at 350° for 30 minutes. Cover and bake 10 minutes more or until dumplings are done. **Yield:** 6-8 servings.

cheese potato puff

Beverly Templeton, Garner, Iowa

I enjoy entertaining and always look for recipes that can be made ahead of time. I got this comforting potato recipe from my mother-in-law. It's wonderful because I can prepare it the night before. It contains basic ingredients that everyone loves like potatoes, milk and cheddar cheese.

- 12 medium potatoes, peeled (about 5 pounds)
- 1 teaspoon salt, *divided*
- 3/4 cup butter
- 2 cups (8 ounces) shredded cheddar cheese
- 1 cup milk
- 2 eggs, beaten

Fresh *or* dried chives, optional

Place potatoes in a large kettle; cover with water. Add 1/2 teaspoon salt; cook until tender. Drain; mash potatoes until smooth.

In a saucepan, cook and stir the butter, cheese, milk and remaining salt until smooth. Stir into the potatoes; fold in eggs.

Pour mixture into a greased 3-qt. baking dish. Bake, uncovered, at 350° for 40 minutes or until puffy and golden brown. Sprinkle with chives if desired. **Yield:** 8-10 servings.

Editor's Note: Casserole may be covered and refrigerated overnight. Allow to stand at room temperature for 30 minutes before baking.

tuna mushroom casserole

Jone Furlong, Santa Rosa, California

I love to serve this dressed-up version of a tuna casserole. The green beans add nice texture, color and flavor.

- 1/2 cup water
- 1 teaspoon chicken bouillon granules
- 1 package (10 ounces) frozen green beans
- 1 cup chopped onion
- 1 cup sliced fresh mushrooms
- 1/4 cup chopped celery
- 1 garlic clove, minced
- 1/2 teaspoon dill weed
- 1/2 teaspoon salt
- 1/8 teaspoon pepper
- 4 teaspoons cornstarch
- 1-1/2 cups milk
- 1/2 cup shredded Swiss cheese
- 1/4 cup mayonnaise
- 2-1/2 cups medium noodles, cooked and drained
- 1 can (12-1/4 ounces) tuna, drained and flaked
- 1/3 cup dry bread crumbs
- 1 tablespoon butter

In a large saucepan, bring water and bouillon to a boil, stirring to dissolve. Add the next eight ingredients; bring to a boil. Reduce heat; cover and simmer 5 minutes or until vegetables are tender. Dissolve cornstarch in milk; add to vegetable mixture, stirring constantly. Bring to a boil; boil 2 minutes or until thickened.

Remove from the heat; stir in cheese and mayonnaise until cheese is melted. Fold in noodles and tuna. Pour into a greased 2-1/2-qt. baking dish. Brown bread crumbs in butter; sprinkle on top of casserole. Bake, uncovered, at 350° for 25-30 minutes or until heated through. **Yield:** 4-6 servings.

cordon bleu casserole

Joyce Paul, Moose Jaw, Saskatchewan
Whenever I'm invited to attend a potluck, people usually ask me to bring this tempting casserole. The turkey, ham and cheese are delectable combined with the crunchy topping.

    4 cups cubed cooked turkey
    3 cups cubed fully cooked ham
    1 cup (4 ounces) shredded cheddar cheese
    1 cup chopped onion
1/4 cup butter
1/3 cup all-purpose flour
    2 cups half-and-half cream
    1 teaspoon dill weed
1/8 teaspoon ground mustard
1/8 teaspoon ground nutmeg
TOPPING:
    1 cup dry bread crumbs
    2 tablespoons butter, melted
1/4 teaspoon dill weed
1/4 cup shredded cheddar cheese
1/4 cup chopped walnuts

In a large bowl, combine turkey, ham and cheese; set aside. In a saucepan, saute onion in butter until tender. Add flour; stir to form a paste. Gradually add cream, stirring constantly. Bring to a boil; boil 1 minute or until thick. Add dill, mustard and nutmeg; mix well. Remove from the heat and pour over meat mixture.

Spoon into a greased 13-in. x 9-in. x 2-in. baking dish. Toss bread crumbs, butter and dill; stir in cheese and walnuts. Sprinkle over the casserole. Bake, uncovered, at 350° for 30 minutes or until heated through. **Yield:** 8-10 servings.

spaghetti squash casserole

Myna Dyck, Boissevain, Manitoba
Spaghetti squash, like zucchini, can take over a backyard garden. This casserole is an excellent way to put that abundance to good use.

    1 small spaghetti squash (1-1/2 to 2 pounds)
1/2 cup water
    1 pound ground beef
1/2 cup chopped onion
1/2 cup chopped sweet red pepper
    1 garlic clove, minced
    1 can (8 ounces) diced tomatoes, undrained
1/2 teaspoon dried oregano
1/4 teaspoon salt
1/8 teaspoon pepper
    1 cup (4 ounces) shredded mozzarella *or* cheddar cheese
    1 tablespoon chopped fresh parsley

Cut squash in half lengthwise; scoop out seeds. Place with cut side down in a baking dish; add water. Cover and bake at 375° for 20-30 minutes or until it is easily pierced with a fork. When cool enough to handle, scoop out squash, separating the strands with a fork.

In a skillet, cook beef, onion, red pepper and garlic until meat is no longer pink and the vegetables are tender. Drain; add tomatoes, oregano, salt, pepper and squash. Cook and stir for 1-2 minutes or until liquid is absorbed. Transfer to an ungreased 1-1/2-qt. baking dish.

Bake, uncovered, at 350° for 25 minutes. Sprinkle with the cheese and parsley; let stand a few minutes. **Yield:** 6-8 servings.

pork and green chili casserole

Dianne Esposite, New Middletown, Ohio

I work at a local hospital and also part time for some area doctors, so I'm always on the lookout for good, quick recipes to fix for my family. Some of my co-workers and I exchange recipes. This zippy casserole is one that was brought to a picnic at my house. People raved over it.

1-1/2 pounds boneless pork, cut into 1/2-inch cubes
    1 tablespoon vegetable oil
    1 can (15 ounces) black beans, rinsed and drained
    1 can (10-3/4 ounces) condensed cream of chicken soup, undiluted
    1 can (14-1/2 ounces) diced tomatoes, undrained
    2 cans (4 ounces *each*) chopped green chilies
    1 cup quick-cooking brown rice
  1/4 cup water
    2 to 3 tablespoons salsa
    1 teaspoon ground cumin
  1/2 cup shredded cheddar cheese

In a large skillet, saute pork in oil until no pink remains; drain. Add the beans, soup, tomatoes, chilies, rice, water, salsa and cumin; cook and stir until bubbly. Pour into an ungreased 2-qt. baking dish.

Bake, uncovered, at 350° for 30 minutes or until bubbly. Sprinkle with cheese; let stand a few minutes before serving. **Yield:** 6 servings.

butternut squash bake

Julie Jahn, Decatur, Indiana

If I ask our two girls what to fix for a special meal, this dish is always requested. I discovered this slightly sweet and crunchy-topped casserole at a church dinner about 20 years ago, and now I take it to potluck dinners and come home with an empty dish! Crisp rice cereal and pecans are unusual but tasty toppings.

  1/3 cup butter, softened
  3/4 cup sugar
    2 eggs
    1 can (5 ounces) evaporated milk
    1 teaspoon vanilla extract
    2 cups mashed cooked butternut squash
TOPPING:
  1/2 cup crisp rice cereal
  1/4 cup packed brown sugar
  1/4 cup chopped pecans
    2 tablespoons butter, melted

In a mixing bowl, cream the butter and sugar. Beat in the eggs, milk and vanilla. Stir in the squash (mixture will be thin). Pour into a greased 11-in. x 7-in. x 2-in. baking pan.

Bake, uncovered, at 350° for 45 minutes or until almost set. Combine topping ingredients; sprinkle over casserole. Return to the oven for 5-10 minutes or until bubbly. **Yield:** 6-8 servings.

lasagna with white sauce

Angie Price, Bradford, Tennessee

I'm an old-fashioned country cook and love preparing recipes like this one that uses staples I normally keep on hand. Unlike most lasagnas, this one doesn't call for precooking the noodles. It's so simple my children sometimes make it after school and have it ready when I get home from work.

- 1 pound ground beef
- 1 large onion, chopped
- 1 can (14-1/2 ounces) diced tomatoes, undrained
- 2 tablespoons tomato paste
- 1 beef bouillon cube
- 1-1/2 teaspoons Italian seasoning
- 1 teaspoon salt
- 1/2 teaspoon pepper
- 1/4 teaspoon ground red *or* cayenne pepper

WHITE SAUCE:
- 2 tablespoons butter
- 3 tablespoons all-purpose flour
- 1 teaspoon salt
- 1/4 teaspoon pepper
- 2 cups milk
- 1-1/4 cups shredded mozzarella cheese, *divided*
- 10 to 12 uncooked lasagna noodles

In a Dutch oven, cook beef and onion until meat is no longer pink and onion is tender; drain. Add tomatoes, tomato paste, bouillon and seasonings. Cover and cook over medium-low heat for 20 minutes, stirring occasionally.

Meanwhile, melt butter in a medium saucepan; stir in flour, salt and pepper. Add milk gradually; bring to a boil, stirring constantly. Reduce heat and cook for 1 minute. Remove from the heat and stir in half of the cheese; set aside.

Pour half of the meat sauce into an ungreased 13-in. x 9-in. x 2-in. baking dish. Cover with half of the lasagna noodles. Cover with remaining meat sauce. Top with remaining noodles. Pour white sauce over noodles. Sprinkle with remaining cheese. Cover and bake at 400° for 40 minutes or until noodles are done. **Yield:** 10-12 servings.

---

prize winning tips

✳ Lasagna takes on a whole different twist if you spread frozen chopped spinach that has been thawed, well drained and squeezed dry on the middle layer. It adds great flavor and color.

Kris Martinell, Dell, Montana

✳ Like a flavorful change of pace? Top your favorite ground beef casserole with butter-flavored cracker crumbs instead of potato chips.

Michelle Gazaw, Wynantskill, New York

✳ Add some dried marjoram the next time you make a creamy ham casserole. It's just the right complement.

Caryn Hasbrouck, Wheaton, Illinois

---

runners-up

monterey spaghetti

Janet Hibler, Cameron, Missouri
I'm a working mother with two young boys. Our family leads a very active life, so I make a lot of casseroles. It's so nice to have a hearty, nutritious side dish the kids will eat. Topped with cheese and french-fried onions, this tasty casserole is a hit at our house.

    4 ounces spaghetti, broken into 2-inch
      pieces
    1 egg
    1 cup (8 ounces) sour cream
  1/4 cup grated Parmesan cheese
  1/4 teaspoon garlic powder
    2 cups (8 ounces) shredded Monterey Jack
      cheese
    1 package (10 ounces) frozen chopped spinach,
      thawed and drained
    1 can (2.8 ounces) french-fried onions, *divided*

Cook the spaghetti according to package directions. Meanwhile, in a medium bowl, beat the egg. Add the sour cream, Parmesan cheese and garlic powder. Drain spaghetti; add to egg mixture with Monterey Jack cheese, spinach and half of the onions. Pour into a greased 2-qt. baking dish.

Cover and bake at 350° for 30 minutes or until heated through. Top with remaining onions; return to the oven for 5 minutes or until onions are golden brown. **Yield:** 6-8 servings.

pan burritos

Joyce Kent, Grand Rapids, Michigan
Our family loves Mexican food, so this flavorful, satisfying casserole is a favorite.

    2 packages (1-1/2 ounces *each*) enchilada
      sauce mix
    3 cups water
    1 can (12 ounces) tomato paste
    1 garlic clove, minced
  1/4 teaspoon pepper
Salt to taste
    2 pounds ground beef
    9 large flour tortillas (9 inches)
    4 cups (16 ounces) shredded cheddar cheese
      or taco cheese
    1 can (16 ounces) refried beans, warmed
Taco sauce, sour cream, chili peppers, chopped
    onion *and/or* guacamole, optional

In a saucepan, combine the first six ingredients; simmer for 15-20 minutes. In a skillet, cook the beef over medium heat until no longer pink. Drain; stir in one-third of the sauce. Spread another third on the bottom of a greased 13-in. x 9-in. x 2-in. baking pan.

Place three tortillas over sauce, tearing to fit bottom of pan. Spoon half of meat mixture over tortillas; sprinkle with 1-1/2 cups cheese. Add three more tortillas. Spread refried beans over tortillas; top with remaining meat. Sprinkle with 1-1/2 cups of cheese. Layer remaining tortillas; top with the remaining sauce. Sprinkle with remaining cheese.

Bake, uncovered, at 350° for 35-40 minutes. Let stand 10 minutes before cutting. Serve with taco sauce, sour cream, chili peppers, chopped onion and/or guacamole if desired. **Yield:** 8-10 servings.

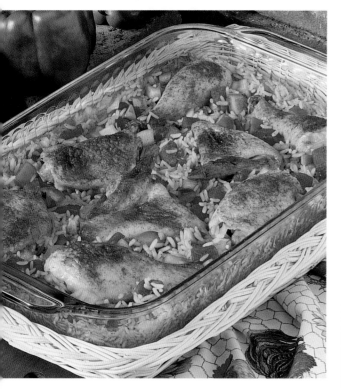

spanish rice and chicken

Cindy Clark, Mechanicsburg, Pennsylvania

My mother has always been an avid cook, and my sister, two brothers and I were raised on this casserole. When I polled our family to see which recipe I should share, this fresh-tasting, well-seasoned chicken casserole came out on the top of the list. I know you'll enjoy it as much as we do.

- 1 broiler/fryer chicken (2-1/2 to 3 pounds), cut up
- 1 teaspoon garlic salt
- 1 teaspoon celery salt
- 1 teaspoon paprika
- 1 cup uncooked rice
- 3/4 cup chopped onion
- 3/4 cup chopped green pepper
- 1/4 cup minced fresh parsley
- 1-1/2 cups chicken broth
- 1 cup chopped tomatoes
- 1-1/2 teaspoons salt
- 1-1/2 teaspoons chili powder

Place chicken in a greased 13-in. x 9-in. x 2-in. baking pan. Combine garlic salt, celery salt and paprika; sprinkle over chicken. Bake, uncovered, at 425° for 20 minutes. Remove chicken from pan. Combine rice, onion, green pepper and parsley; spoon into the pan.

In a saucepan, bring broth, tomatoes, salt and chili powder to a boil. Pour over rice mixture; mix well. Place chicken pieces on top. Cover and bake for 45 minutes or until chicken and rice are tender. **Yield:** 4-6 servings.

hungarian noodle side dish

Betty Sugg, Akron, New York

I first served this creamy, rich casserole at our ladies meeting at church. Everyone liked it and many of the ladies wanted the recipe. The original recipe was from a friend, but I changed it a bit to suit our tastes.

- 3 chicken bouillon cubes
- 1/4 cup boiling water
- 1 can (10-3/4 ounces) condensed cream of mushroom soup, undiluted
- 1/2 cup chopped onion
- 2 tablespoons Worcestershire sauce
- 2 tablespoons poppy seeds
- 1/8 to 1/4 teaspoon garlic powder
- 1/8 to 1/4 teaspoon hot pepper sauce
- 2 cups (16 ounces) cottage cheese
- 2 cups (16 ounces) sour cream
- 1 package (16 ounces) medium noodles, cooked and drained
- 1/4 cup shredded Parmesan cheese

Paprika

In a large bowl, dissolve bouillon in water. Add the next six ingredients; mix well. Stir in cottage cheese, sour cream and noodles and mix well. Pour into a greased 2-1/2-qt. baking dish. Sprinkle with the Parmesan cheese and paprika. Cover and bake at 350° for 45 minutes or until heated through. **Yield:** 8-10 servings.

Editor's Note: Casserole may be covered and refrigerated overnight. Allow to stand at room temperature for 30 minutes before baking.

SLOW-COOKED SPECIALTIES

#1

TANGY PORK CHOPS

tangy pork chops

Clever cooks who take advantage of a slow cooker know the joy of coming into the kitchen after a busy day away to find a hot, delicious meal waiting.

In addition to handy main-dish preparation, slow cookers can also serve up a no-fuss soup, side dish or dessert. In our Slow-Cooked Specialties contest, subscribers entered 3,500 of their favorites. Your slow cooker may take its time with any of the 12 winners featured here, but your family will be sure to gobble them up fast!

"Fancy enough for company, these mouth-watering pork chops also make a great family meal."

Tangy Pork Chops from Karol Hines of Kitty Hawk, North Carolina took the Grand Prize. "Fancy enough for company, these mouth-watering pork chops also make a great family meal," say Karol. "I usually have all the ingredients on hand. When my husband and I had our first child, this recipe was so convenient—I started it during naptime for a no-fuss supper later."

  4 **pork chops (1/2 inch thick)**
1/2 **teaspoon salt**
1/8 **teaspoon pepper**
  2 **medium onions, chopped**
  2 **celery ribs, chopped**
  1 **large green pepper, sliced**
  1 **can (14-1/2 ounces) stewed tomatoes**
1/2 **cup ketchup**
  2 **tablespoons cider vinegar**
  2 **tablespoons brown sugar**
  2 **tablespoons Worcestershire sauce**
  1 **tablespoon lemon juice**
  1 **beef bouillon cube**
  2 **tablespoons cornstarch**
  2 **tablespoons water**
Hot cooked rice, optional

Place chops in a slow cooker; sprinkle with salt and pepper. Add the onions, celery, green pepper and tomatoes. Combine ketchup, vinegar, sugar, Worcestershire sauce, lemon juice and bouillon; pour over vegetables. Cover and cook on low for 5-6 hours.

Mix cornstarch and water until smooth; stir into liquid in slow cooker. Cover and cook on high for 30 minutes or until thickened. Serve over rice if desired. **Yield:** 4 servings.

stuffed chicken rolls

Jean Sherwood, Kenneth City, Florida
The wonderful aroma of this moist, delicious chicken cooking sparks our appetites. The ham and cheese rolled inside is a tasty surprise. When I prepared this impressive main dish for a church luncheon, I received lots of compliments. The rolls are especially nice served over rice or pasta.

    6 large boneless skinless chicken breast halves
    6 slices fully cooked ham
    6 slices Swiss cheese
    1/4 cup all-purpose flour
    1/4 cup grated Parmesan cheese
    1/2 teaspoon rubbed sage
    1/4 teaspoon paprika
    1/4 teaspoon pepper
    1/4 cup vegetable oil
    1 can (10-3/4 ounces) condensed cream of
        chicken soup, undiluted
    1/2 cup chicken broth
Chopped fresh parsley, optional

Flatten chicken to 1/8-in. thickness. Place ham and cheese on each breast. Roll up and tuck in ends; secure with a toothpick. Combine the flour, Parmesan cheese, sage, paprika and pepper; coat chicken on all sides. Cover and refrigerate for 1 hour.

In a large skillet, brown chicken in oil over medium-high heat. Transfer to a 5-qt. slow cooker. Combine soup and broth; pour over chicken. Cover and cook on low for 4-5 hours. Remove toothpicks. Garnish with parsley if desired. **Yield:** 6 servings.

teriyaki sandwiches

Bernice Muilenburg, Molalla, Oregon
The meat for these sandwiches comes out of the slow cooker tender and flavorful. Living as we do in the foothills of the Cascades, we frequently have deer and elk in the freezer. I sometimes substitute that in this recipe, and it never tastes like game.

    2 pounds boneless chuck steak
    1/4 cup soy sauce
    1 tablespoon brown sugar
    1 teaspoon ground ginger
    1 garlic clove, minced
    4 teaspoons cornstarch
    2 tablespoons water
    8 French rolls, split
    1/4 cup butter, melted
Pineapple rings
Chopped green onions

Cut steak into thin bite-size slices. In a slow cooker, combine soy sauce, sugar, ginger and garlic. Add steak. Cover and cook on low for 7-9 hours or until meat is tender.

Remove meat with a slotted spoon; set aside. Carefully pour liquid into a 2-cup measuring cup; skim fat. Add water to liquid to measure 1-1/2 cups. Pour into a large saucepan. Combine cornstarch and water until smooth; add to pan. Cook and stir until thick and bubbly, about 2 minutes. Add meat and heat through.

Brush rolls with butter; broil 4-5 in. from the heat for 2-3 minutes or until lightly toasted. Fill with meat, pineapple and green onions. **Yield:** 8 servings.

nutty apple streusel dessert

Jacki Every, Rotterdam, New York
Many people don't think of using a slow cooker to make dessert, but I like finishing up our dinner and having this hot, scrumptious apple treat waiting to be served up. I can start it in the morning and not think about it all day.

  6 cups sliced peeled tart apples
1-1/4 teaspoons ground cinnamon
 1/4 teaspoon ground allspice
 1/4 teaspoon ground nutmeg
 3/4 cup milk
  2 tablespoons butter, softened
 3/4 cup sugar
  2 eggs
  1 teaspoon vanilla extract
 1/2 cup biscuit/baking mix
TOPPING:
  1 cup biscuit/baking mix
 1/3 cup packed brown sugar
  3 tablespoons cold butter
 1/2 cup sliced almonds
Ice cream or whipped cream, optional

In a large bowl, toss apples with cinnamon, allspice and nutmeg. Place in a greased slow cooker. In a mixing bowl, combine milk, butter, sugar, eggs, vanilla and baking mix; mix well. Spoon over apples.

For topping, combine biscuit mix and brown sugar in a bowl; cut in butter until crumbly. Add almonds; sprinkle over apples. Cover and cook on low for 6-7 hours or until the apples are tender. Serve with ice cream or whipped cream if desired. **Yield:** 6-8 servings.

hearty new england dinner

Claire McCombs, San Diego, California
This favorite slow-cooker recipe came from a friend. The horseradish in the gravy adds zip.

  2 medium carrots, sliced
  1 medium onion, sliced
  1 celery rib, sliced
  1 boneless chuck roast (about 3 pounds)
  1 teaspoon salt, *divided*
 1/4 teaspoon pepper
  1 envelope onion soup mix
  2 cups water
  1 tablespoon vinegar
  1 bay leaf
 1/2 small head cabbage, cut into wedges
  3 tablespoons butter
  2 tablespoons all-purpose flour
  1 tablespoon dried minced onion
  2 tablespoons prepared horseradish

Place carrots, onion and celery in a 5-qt. slow cooker. Place the roast on top; sprinkle with 1/2 teaspoon salt and pepper. Add soup mix, water, vinegar and bay leaf. Cover and cook on low for 7-9 hours or until beef is tender.

Remove beef and keep warm; discard bay leaf. Add cabbage. Cover and cook on high for 30-40 minutes or until cabbage is tender.

Meanwhile, melt butter in a small saucepan; stir in flour and onion. Add 1-1/2 cups cooking liquid from the slow cooker. Stir in horseradish and remaining salt; bring to a boil. Cook and stir over low heat until thick and smooth, about 2 minutes. Serve with roast and vegetables. **Yield:** 6-8 servings.

egg and broccoli casserole

Janet Sliter, Kennewick, Washington

For years, I've prepared this filling egg casserole —which is delicious for brunch—in my slow cooker. It's an unusual recipe for this appliance but is welcomed wherever I serve it. Folks always go back for second and third helpings.

- 1 carton (24 ounces) small-curd cottage cheese
- 1 package (10 ounces) frozen chopped broccoli, thawed and drained
- 2 cups (8 ounces) shredded cheddar cheese
- 6 eggs, beaten
- 1/3 cup all-purpose flour
- 1/4 cup butter, melted
- 3 tablespoons finely chopped onion
- 1/2 teaspoon salt
- Additional shredded cheddar cheese, optional

In a large bowl, combine the first eight ingredients. Pour into a greased slow cooker. Cover and cook on high for 1 hour.

Stir. Reduce heat to low; cover and cook 2-1/2 to 3 hours longer or until a thermometer placed in the center reads 160° and the eggs are set. Sprinkle with additional cheese if desired. **Yield:** 6 servings.

partytime beans

Jean Cantner, Boston, Virginia

A friend brought this colorful bean dish to my house for a church circle potluck dinner a number of years ago. As soon as I tasted these slightly sweet baked beans, I had to have the recipe. I've served this and shared the recipe many times since.

- 1-1/2 cups ketchup
- 1 medium onion, chopped
- 1 medium green pepper, chopped
- 1 medium sweet red pepper, chopped
- 1/2 cup water
- 1/2 cup packed brown sugar
- 2 bay leaves
- 2 to 3 teaspoons cider vinegar
- 1 teaspoon ground mustard
- 1/8 teaspoon pepper
- 1 can (16 ounces) kidney beans, rinsed and drained
- 1 can (15-1/2 ounces) great northern beans, rinsed and drained
- 1 can (15 ounces) lima beans, rinsed and drained
- 1 can (15 ounces) black beans, rinsed and drained
- 1 can (15-1/2 ounces) black-eyed peas, rinsed and drained

In a slow cooker, combine the first 10 ingredients; mix well. Add the beans and peas; mix well. Cover and cook on low for 5-7 hours or until onion and peppers are tender. Remove bay leaves. **Yield:** 14-16 servings.

black and blue cobbler

Martha Creveling, Orlando, Florida

It never occurred to me that I could bake a cobbler in my slow cooker until I saw some recipes and decided to try my favorite fruity dessert recipe. It took a bit of experimenting, but the results are "berry" well worth it.

    1 cup all-purpose flour
1-1/2 cups sugar, *divided*
    1 teaspoon baking powder
  1/4 teaspoon salt
  1/4 teaspoon ground cinnamon
  1/4 teaspoon ground nutmeg
    2 eggs, beaten
    2 tablespoons milk
    2 tablespoons vegetable oil
    2 cups fresh *or* frozen blackberries
    2 cups fresh *or* frozen blueberries
  3/4 cup water
    1 teaspoon grated orange peel
Whipped cream *or* ice cream, optional

In a bowl, combine flour, 3/4 cup sugar, baking powder, salt, cinnamon and nutmeg. Combine eggs, milk and oil; stir into dry ingredients just until moistened. Spread the batter evenly onto the bottom of a greased 5-qt. slow cooker.

In a saucepan, combine berries, water, orange peel and remaining sugar; bring to a boil. Remove from the heat; immediately pour over batter. Cover and cook on high for 2 to 2-1/2 hours or until a toothpick inserted into the batter comes out clean.

Turn cooker off. Uncover and let stand for 30 minutes before serving. Serve with whipped cream or ice cream if desired. **Yield:** 6 servings.

prize winning tips

* * * * *

*To avoid heating up your kitchen during the hot summer months, try cooking pot roast in a slow cooker. All you lose is extra heat!

Caroline Christensen, Richfield, Utah

*Economical, less-tender cuts of beef like round steak, stew meat and cube steak are perfect for the slow cooker. The long, slow cooking process ensures fork-tender, moist and flavorful meat even on cuts that would be tough and chewy prepared using other cooking methods. For meats to cook evenly in the slow cooker, allow some space between the pieces so the heat can circulate.

Teona Miller, Phoenix, Arizona

*For a super-easy slow cooker recipe, try adding a couple envelopes of Italian salad dressing mix to a roast, and nothing else.

Sharon Wilging, Mountain, Wisconsin

runners-up

slow-cooker enchiladas

Mary Luebbert, Benton, Kansas
As a busy wife and mother of two young sons, I rely on this handy recipe. I layer enchilada ingredients in the slow cooker, turn it on and forget about it. With a bit of spice, these hearty enchiladas are especially nice during the colder months.

- 1 pound ground beef
- 1 cup chopped onion
- 1/2 cup chopped green pepper
- 1 can (16 ounces) pinto *or* kidney beans, rinsed and drained
- 1 can (15 ounces) black beans, rinsed and drained
- 1 can (10 ounces) diced tomatoes and green chilies, undrained
- 1/3 cup water
- 1 teaspoon chili powder
- 1/2 teaspoon ground cumin
- 1/2 teaspoon salt
- 1/4 teaspoon pepper
- 1 cup (4 ounces) shredded sharp cheddar cheese
- 1 cup (4 ounces) shredded Monterey Jack cheese
- 6 flour tortillas (6 *or* 7 inches)

In a skillet, cook beef, onion and green pepper until beef is no longer pink and vegetables are tender; drain. Add next eight ingredients; bring to a boil. Reduce heat; cover and simmer for 10 minutes. Combine cheeses.

In a 5-qt. slow cooker, layer about 3/4 cup beef mixture, one tortilla and about 1/3 cup cheese. Repeat layers. Cover and cook on low for 5-7 hours or until heated through. **Yield:** 4 servings.

championship bean dip

Wendi Wavrin Law, Omaha, Nebraska
My friends and neighbors always expect me to bring this irresistible dip to every gathering. When I arrive, they ask, "You brought your bean dip along, didn't you?" If there are any leftovers, we use them to make bean and cheese burritos the next day. I've given out this recipe a hundred times.

- 1 can (16 ounces) refried beans
- 1 cup picante sauce
- 1 cup (4 ounces) shredded Monterey Jack cheese
- 1 cup (4 ounces) shredded cheddar cheese
- 3/4 cup sour cream
- 1 package (3 ounces) cream cheese, softened
- 1 tablespoon chili powder
- 1/4 teaspoon ground cumin

Tortilla chips

Salsa

In a large bowl, combine the first eight ingredients, then transfer to a slow cooker. Cover and cook on high for 2 hours or until the dip is heated through, stirring once or twice. Serve with tortilla chips and salsa. **Yield:** 4-1/2 cups.

sesame pork ribs

Sandy Alexander, Fayetteville, North Carolina
No one ever believes how little effort it takes to make these tender, juicy country-style ribs. The flavor of the lightly sweet and tangy sauce penetrates through the meat as the ribs simmer in the slow cooker all day.

    3/4 cup packed brown sugar
    1/2 cup soy sauce
    1/2 cup ketchup
    1/4 cup honey
      2 tablespoons white wine vinegar
      3 garlic cloves, minced
      1 teaspoon ground ginger
      1 teaspoon salt
    1/4 to 1/2 teaspoon crushed red pepper flakes
      5 pounds country-style pork ribs
      1 medium onion, sliced
      2 tablespoons sesame seeds, toasted
      2 tablespoons chopped green onions

In a large bowl, combine the first nine ingredients. Add ribs and turn to coat. Place the onion in a 5-qt. slow cooker; arrange ribs on top and pour sauce over.

Cover and cook on low for 5-6 hours or until a meat thermometer reads 160°-170°. Place ribs on a serving platter; sprinkle with sesame seeds and green onions. **Yield:** 6 servings.

texican chili

Stacy Law, Cornish, Utah
This flavorful, meaty chili is my favorite…and it's so easy to prepare in the slow cooker. It's a great way to serve a crowd without last-minute preparation. I got the idea from my mother, who used her slow cooker often for soups and stews.

      8 bacon strips, diced
    2-1/2 pounds beef stew meat, cut into 1/2-inch
          cubes
      2 cans (one 28 ounces, one 14-1/2 ounces)
          stewed tomatoes
      2 cans (8 ounces *each*) tomato sauce
      1 can (16 ounces) kidney beans, rinsed and
          drained
      2 cups sliced carrots
      1 medium onion, chopped
      1 cup chopped celery
    1/2 cup chopped green pepper
    1/4 cup minced fresh parsley
      1 tablespoon chili powder
      1 teaspoon salt
    1/2 teaspoon ground cumin
    1/4 teaspoon pepper

In a skillet, cook bacon until crisp. Remove to paper towel to drain. Brown beef in the drippings over medium heat; drain. Transfer to a 5-qt. slow cooker; add bacon and remaining ingredients. Cover and cook on low for 9-10 hours or until the meat is tender, stirring occasionally. **Yield:** 16-18 servings.

GREAT GRILLING

#1

PORK WITH TANGY
MUSTARD SAUCE

pork with tangy mustard sauce

GRAND PRIZE WINNER

I f you can't stand the heat, get out of the kitchen. When the weather is too warm, many cooks heed that sage advice by heading outdoors to the grill. Our Test Kitchen staff got fired up to do the same.

> "As it's cooking, the aroma of the pork is mouth-watering..."

Their goal was to grill up dozens of family favorite dishes from among the thousands entered in our Great Grilling contest—and the competition was hot!

When the smoke cleared, our panel of judges had sampled savory grilled ribs, roasts, kabobs, burgers, chicken, fish and more. After comparing notes, they agreed the Grand Prize should go to Ginger Johnson of Farmington, Illinois for her flavorful Pork with Tangy Mustard Sauce.

"Everyone who's tried it loves the bite of the mustard horseradish sauce mixed with the sweet-sour taste of the preserves," says Ginger. "As it's cooking, the aroma of the pork is mouth-watering, and the sauce forms a crusty glaze that is so appetizing."

1 boneless pork loin roast (2-1/2 to 3 pounds)
2 teaspoons olive oil
1-1/4 teaspoons ground mustard
3/4 teaspoon garlic powder
1/4 teaspoon ground ginger
1/2 cup horseradish mustard
1/2 cup apricot *or* pineapple preserves

Rub roast with oil. Combine mustard, garlic powder and ginger; rub over roast. Place in a large resealable plastic bag or shallow glass container; seal bag or cover container. Refrigerate overnight.

Grill roast, covered, over indirect heat for 60 minutes. Combine the horseradish mustard and preserves. Continue grilling for 15-30 minutes, basting twice with sauce, or until a meat thermometer reads 160°-170°. Let stand for 10 minutes before slicing. Heat remaining sauce to serve with roast. **Yield:** 10-12 servings.

Editor's Note: As a substitute for the horseradish mustard, combine 1/4 cup spicy brown mustard and 1/4 cup prepared horseradish.

grilled cheese loaf

Debbi Baker, Green Springs, Ohio
Generally, I serve this with steaks and salads. The loaf's so quick to make, in fact, I often grill two of them.

- 1 package (3 ounces) cream cheese, softened
- 2 tablespoons butter, softened
- 1 cup (4 ounces) shredded mozzarella cheese
- 1/4 cup chopped green onions with tops
- 1/2 teaspoon garlic salt
- 1 loaf (1 pound) French bread, sliced

In a mixing bowl, beat cream cheese and butter. Add cheese, onions and garlic salt; mix well. Spread on both sides of each slice of bread. Wrap loaf in a large piece of heavy-duty foil (about 28 in. x 18 in.); seal tightly.

Grill, covered, over medium heat for 8-10 minutes, turning once. Unwrap foil; grill 5 minutes longer. **Yield:** 10-12 servings.

> *I could never get my ribs tender enough on the grill, until I tried precooking them in a slow cooker on high heat for 2 to 3 hours. Since racks of ribs don't fit in a slow cooker very well, I roll them up and place them in the pot standing up.
>
> Loyda Coulombe, Federal Way, Washington

barbecued spareribs

Jane Uphoff, Idalia, Colorado
All of us—my husband, our two sons and I—love to eat barbecued ribs. But the closest rib restaurant to us is in Denver, 150 miles away. So I came up with this recipe. It's now our traditional meal on the Fourth of July.

- 1 tablespoon ground mustard
- 1 tablespoon chili powder
- 1/2 teaspoon cayenne pepper
- 1/4 teaspoon garlic powder
- 3 pounds pork spareribs
- 2/3 cup ketchup
- 1/2 cup water
- 1/2 cup chopped onion
- 1/4 cup lemon juice
- 2 tablespoons vegetable oil
- 1 teaspoon dried oregano
- 1 teaspoon Liquid Smoke, optional
- 1/2 teaspoon salt
- 1/4 teaspoon pepper

Combine the first four ingredients; rub over ribs. For sauce, combine the remaining ingredients; mix well and set aside.

Grill ribs, covered, over indirect heat and medium-low heat for 1 hour, turning occasionally. Add 10 briquettes to coals. Grill 30 minutes longer, basting both sides several times with sauce, or until meat is tender. **Yield:** 4 servings.

marinated catfish fillets

Pauletta Boese, Macon, Mississippi
A number of years ago, we hosted a group of young people from Canada. Since we wanted to give them a taste of the South, this was served. They raved about it.

- 6 catfish fillets (about 8 ounces *each*)
- 1 bottle (16 ounces) Italian salad dressing
- 1 can (10-3/4 ounces) condensed tomato soup, undiluted
- 3/4 cup vegetable oil
- 3/4 cup sugar
- 1/3 cup vinegar
- 3/4 teaspoon celery seed
- 3/4 teaspoon salt
- 3/4 teaspoon pepper
- 3/4 teaspoon ground mustard
- 1/2 teaspoon garlic powder

Place fillets in a large resealable plastic bag or shallow glass container; cover with salad dressing. Seal bag or cover container; refrigerate for 1 hour, turning occasionally. Drain and discard marinade.

Combine remaining ingredients; mix well. Remove 1 cup for basting. (Refrigerate remaining sauce for another use.) Grill fillets, covered, over medium-hot heat for 3 minutes on each side. Brush with the basting sauce. Continue grilling for 6-8 minutes or until fish flakes easily with a fork, turning once and basting several times. **Yield:** 6 servings.

Editor's Note: Reserved sauce may be used to brush on grilled or broiled fish, chicken, turkey or pork.

teriyaki beef kabobs

Lisa Hector, Estevan, Saskatchewan
Several years back, my sister-in-law brought this recipe on a family camping trip and we fixed it for an outdoor potluck. It was so delicious that I asked if I could have a copy. It's become a summer standard for us. Making this dish is a team effort...I put the ingredients together, and my husband handles the grilling.

- 1/4 cup vegetable oil
- 1/4 cup orange juice
- 1/4 cup soy sauce
- 1 teaspoon garlic powder
- 1 teaspoon ground ginger
- 1-3/4 pounds beef tenderloin, cut into 1-inch cubes
- 3/4 pound cherry tomatoes
- 1/2 pound fresh whole mushrooms
- 2 large green peppers, cubed
- 1 large red onion, cut into wedges

Hot cooked rice, optional

In a resealable plastic bag or shallow glass container, combine the first five ingredients and mix well. Reserve 1/2 cup for basting and refrigerate. Add beef to remaining marinade; turn to coat. Seal bag or cover container; refrigerate for 1 hour, turning occasionally. Drain and discard the marinade.

On metal or soaked bamboo skewers, alternate beef, tomatoes, mushrooms, green peppers and onions. Grill, uncovered, over medium heat for 3 minutes on each side. Baste with reserved marinade. Continue turning and basting for 8-10 minutes or until meat reaches desired doneness (for rare, a meat thermometer should read 140°; medium, 160°; well-done, 170°). Serve the meat and vegetables over rice if desired. **Yield:** 6-8 servings.

barbecued chuck roast

Ardis Gautier, Lamont, Oklahoma

Whether I serve this roast for church dinners, company or just family, it is always a hit. To go along with it, my family likes scalloped potatoes, tossed salad and pie. If there's ever any left over, it makes good sandwiches, too.

- 1/3 cup cider vinegar
- 1/4 cup ketchup
- 2 tablespoons vegetable oil
- 2 tablespoons soy sauce
- 1 tablespoon Worcestershire sauce
- 1 teaspoon garlic powder
- 1 teaspoon prepared mustard
- 1 teaspoon salt
- 1/4 teaspoon pepper
- 1 boneless chuck roast (2-1/2 to 3 pounds)
- 1/2 cup applesauce

In a large resealable plastic bag or shallow glass container, combine the first nine ingredients; mix well. Add roast and turn to coat. Seal bag or cover container; refrigerate for at least 3 hours, turning occasionally.

Remove roast. Pour marinade into a small saucepan; bring to a boil. Reduce heat; simmer for 15 minutes.

Meanwhile, grill roast, covered, over indirect heat for 20 minutes, turning occasionally. Add applesauce to marinade; brush over roast. Continue basting and turning the roast several times for 1 to 1-1/2 hours or until meat reaches desired doneness (for rare, a meat thermometer should read 140°; medium, 160°; well-done, 170°). **Yield:** 6-8 servings.

maple-glazed chicken wings

Janice Henck, Clarkston, Georgia

Some wonderful maple syrup I brought back from my last trip to Vermont is what inspired my recipe. These wings have been a hit with family and friends. They're very versatile—use them for TV snacks, hors d'oeuvres for parties or showers, or appetizers…or double or triple the recipe and make the wings a main dish you can serve with a salad or corn on the cob on the side.

- 2 to 3 pounds whole chicken wings
- 1 cup maple syrup
- 2/3 cup chili sauce
- 1/2 cup finely chopped onion
- 2 tablespoons Dijon mustard
- 2 teaspoons Worcestershire sauce
- 1/4 to 1/2 teaspoon crushed red pepper flakes

Cut chicken wings into three sections; discard wing tip section. In a large resealable plastic bag or shallow glass container, combine remaining ingredients. Reserve 1 cup for basting and refrigerate.

Add chicken to the remaining marinade and turn to coat. Seal the bag or cover the container; refrigerate for 4 hours, turning occasionally. Drain and discard the marinade.

Grill chicken, covered, over medium heat for 12-16 minutes, turning occasionally. Brush with reserved marinade. Grill, uncovered, for 8-10 minutes or until juices run clear, basting and turning several times. **Yield:** 6-8 servings.

Editor's Note: Instead of being grilled, the chicken wings may be baked in a 375° oven for 30-40 minutes or until juices run clear.

pizza on the grill

Lisa Boettcher, Columbus, Wisconsin

Pizza is such a favorite at our house I make it at least once a week. When the heat and humidity are up there, though, the last thing that I want to do is turn on the oven. So I just move my recipe to the grill—the barbecue flavor mingling with the cheese tastes delicious.

CRUST:
- 1 package (1/4 ounce) active dry yeast
- 1 cup warm water (110° to 115°)
- 2 tablespoons vegetable oil
- 2 teaspoons sugar
- 1 teaspoon baking soda
- 1 teaspoon salt
- 2-3/4 to 3 cups all-purpose flour

TOPPINGS:
- 2 cups cubed cooked chicken
- 1/2 to 3/4 cup barbecue sauce
- 1/2 cup julienned green pepper
- 2 cups (8 ounces) shredded Monterey Jack cheese

In a mixing bowl, dissolve yeast in water. Add the oil, sugar, baking soda, salt and 2 cups flour. Stir in enough remaining flour to form a soft dough. Turn onto a floured surface; knead until smooth and elastic, about 6-8 minutes. Cover and let rest for 10 minutes.

On a floured surface, roll dough into a 13-in. circle. Transfer to a greased 12-in. pizza pan. Build up edges slightly. Grill, covered, over medium heat for 5 minutes.

Remove from the grill.

Combine chicken and barbecue sauce; spread over the crust. Sprinkle with green pepper and cheese. Grill, covered, 5-10 minutes longer or until crust is golden and cheese is melted. **Yield:** 4 servings.

---

prize winning tips

✱ When making hamburger patties, place them on waxed paper on a tray. Once you start grilling, you can just lift the corner of the waxed paper to easily remove them.
Ruth Ann Miller, Sugarcreek, Ohio

✱ If you coat the grill rack with nonstick cooking spray first, there isn't much scrubbing to do after grilling.
Anne McKay, Oliver, British Columbia

✱ Presoak wooden or bamboo skewers in water for at least 20 minutes before threading with meat, vegetables or fruit to prevent them from scorching or burning.
Sally Hook, Houston, Texas

✱ Open foil packets cautiously to let steam escape and prevent burns.
Alice Loen, Starbuck, Minnesota

campfire bundles

Lauri Krause, Jackson, Nebraska

A family camping trip's where I "invented" this recipe. I'd brought along a hodgepodge of ingredients, so I just threw them all together. Everyone said that the bundles were delicious. Ever since, I've also grilled them at home. I also prepare them often for our Ladies' Home Extension meetings.

- 1 large sweet onion, sliced
- 1 large green pepper, sliced
- 1 large sweet red pepper, sliced
- 1 large sweet yellow pepper, sliced
- 4 medium potatoes, sliced 1/2 inch thick
- 6 medium carrots, sliced 1/4 inch thick
- 1 small cabbage, sliced
- 2 medium tomatoes, chopped
- 1 to 1-1/2 pounds fully cooked kielbasa *or* Polish sausage, cut into 1/2-inch pieces
- 1/2 cup butter
- 1 teaspoon salt
- 1/2 teaspoon pepper

Place the vegetables in the order listed on three pieces of double-layered heavy-duty foil (about 18 in. x 18 in.). Add the sausage; dot with butter. Sprinkle with salt and pepper. Fold foil around the mixture and seal tightly.

Grill, covered, over medium heat for 30 minutes. Turn and grill 30 minutes longer or until vegetables are tender. **Yield:** 6 servings.

hawaiian honey burgers

Sheryl Creech, Lancaster, California

These burgers were a favorite when I was growing up. I now use them as a way to "fancy up" a barbecue without a lot of extra preparation. They keep me out of a hot kitchen yet let me serve a nice meal. Fresh fruit and corn on the cob are wonderful accompaniments. As the oldest of six children, I began cooking when I was very young. But I really started enjoying cooking when I married a very appreciative husband. He inspires me!

- 1/2 cup honey
- 1/4 teaspoon ground cinnamon
- 1/4 teaspoon paprika
- 1/4 teaspoon curry powder
- 1/8 teaspoon ground ginger
- 1/8 teaspoon ground nutmeg
- 2 pounds ground beef
- 1/4 cup soy sauce
- 1 can (23 ounces) sliced pineapple, drained
- 8 hamburger buns, split and toasted

Lettuce leaves, optional

In a bowl, combine the first six ingredients; crumble beef over mixture and mix well. Shape into eight 3/4-in.-thick patties. Grill the burgers, uncovered, over medium-hot heat for 3 minutes on each side. Brush with soy sauce. Continue grilling for 4-6 minutes or until juices run clear, basting and turning several times.

During the last 4 minutes, grill the pineapple slices until browned, turning once. Serve burgers and pineapple on buns with lettuce if desired. **Yield:** 8 servings.

pork and apple skewers

Cheryl Plainte, Minot, North Dakota

Necessity was the "mother" of this recipe! I'd already marinated the pork before realizing we were short on kabob vegetables. In place of them, I used apples I had on hand. This has since become one of my most requested dishes. I have prepared these tangy skewers for just the two of us and for friends.

      3/4 **cup barbecue sauce**
      1/2 **cup pineapple juice**
      1/4 **cup honey mustard**
      1/4 **cup packed brown sugar**
        2 **tablespoons soy sauce**
        2 **tablespoons olive oil**
    1-1/2 **pounds pork tenderloin, cut into 3/4-inch cubes**
        5 **medium unpeeled tart apples**

In a large resealable plastic bag or shallow glass container, combine the first six ingredients; mix well. Reserve 1/2 cup for basting and refrigerate. Add pork to remaining marinade and turn to coat. Seal bag or cover container; refrigerate for at least 1 hour.

Drain and discard marinade. Cut the apples into 1-1/2-in. cubes. Alternate pork and apples on metal or soaked bamboo skewers. Grill, uncovered, over medium heat for 3 minutes on each side. Baste with the reserved marinade. Continue turning and basting for 8-10 minutes or until meat juices run clear and apples are tender. **Yield:** 6 servings.

Editor's Note: As a substitute for honey mustard, combine 2 tablespoons Dijon mustard and 2 tablespoons honey.

spicy grilled chicken

Edith Maki, Hancock, Michigan

Very near the top of the list of foods I prepare for company is this chicken. It's easy to fix and has never flopped. It is a family favorite, too—any leftovers are great in a salad or sandwich.

      3/4 **cup finely chopped onion**
      1/2 **cup grapefruit juice**
        2 **tablespoons olive oil**
        2 **tablespoons soy sauce**
        1 **tablespoon honey**
        1 **garlic clove, minced**
    1-1/2 **teaspoons salt**
    1-1/2 **teaspoons rubbed sage**
    1-1/2 **teaspoons dried thyme**
        1 **teaspoon ground allspice**
        1 **teaspoon garlic powder**
      1/2 **teaspoon ground cinnamon**
      1/2 **teaspoon ground nutmeg**
      1/4 **teaspoon cayenne pepper**
      1/4 **teaspoon pepper**
        6 **boneless skinless chicken breast halves**

In a large resealable plastic bag or shallow glass container, combine the first 15 ingredients; mix well. Reserve 1/3 cup for basting and refrigerate. Add chicken to remaining marinade and turn to coat. Seal bag or cover container; refrigerate overnight.

Drain and discard marinade. Grill chicken, uncovered, over medium heat for 3 minutes on each side. Baste with reserved marinade. Continue grilling for 6-8 minutes or until juices run clear, basting and turning several times. **Yield:** 6 servings.

SENSATIONAL SOUPS
#1

NEIGHBORHOOD
BEAN SOUP

neighborhood bean soup

Cooking can't get much more "country" than hearty, homemade soups. And soups can't get much more satisfying than the flavorful and filling fare simmered up in our Sensational Soups contest!

As they spooned their bowls clean to the bottom, our judges jotted down their impressions. Later, when notes were compared, one standout stood at the top of everyone's list—Neighborhood Bean Soup from Cheryl Trowbridge of Windsor, Ontario.

"Several neighbor ladies really enjoy this soup, and I love sharing it with them."

Says Cheryl about her Grand Prize Winner, "Several neighbor ladies really enjoy this soup, and I love sharing it with them. In fact, each leaves her own personal container in my pantry so I can ladle it full when I make a batch. After that's done, there are just a couple of servings left for me and my father."

Prepare a pot of her soup soon and you'll know why it's in demand. Better be sure, though, to make a big batch—in case the neighbors catch a whiff!

2 cups dried great northern beans
5 cups chicken broth
3 cups water
1 large meaty ham bone
2 to 3 tablespoons chicken bouillon granules
1 teaspoon dried thyme
1/2 teaspoon dried marjoram
1/2 teaspoon pepper
1/4 teaspoon rubbed sage
1/4 teaspoon dried savory
2 medium onions, chopped
3 medium carrots, chopped
3 celery ribs, chopped
1 tablespoon vegetable oil

Place beans in a Dutch oven or soup kettle; add water to cover by 2 in. Bring to a boil; boil for 2 minutes. Remove from the heat; cover and let stand for 1 hour.

Drain. Add broth, water, ham bone, bouillon and seasonings; bring to a boil. Reduce heat; cover and simmer for 2 hours.

Saute onions, carrots and celery in oil; add to soup. Cover and simmer 1 hour longer. Debone ham and cut into chunks; return to the soup. Skim fat. **Yield:** 10 servings (2-3/4 quarts).

marvelous mushroom soup

Beverly Rafferty, Winston, Oregon
Soup is tops on the list of things I love to cook. I've used this one as the beginning course to a meal…and as a Sunday supper with hot rolls and butter. When we had a small restaurant in Arizona, I made my mushroom soup every day. We never had any left over. It got raves at a deli I worked at, too.

- 1/2 **pound fresh mushrooms, sliced**
- 1 **large onion, finely chopped**
- 1 **garlic clove, minced**
- 1/2 **teaspoon dried tarragon**
- 1/4 **teaspoon ground nutmeg**
- 3 **tablespoons butter**
- 1/4 **cup all-purpose flour**
- 2 **cans (14-1/2 ounces *each*) beef broth**
- 1 **cup (8 ounces) sour cream**
- 1/2 **cup half-and-half cream**
- 1/2 **cup evaporated milk**
- 1 **teaspoon lemon juice**
Dash hot pepper sauce
Salt and pepper to taste

In a Dutch oven or soup kettle, saute the mushrooms, onion, garlic, tarragon and nutmeg in butter until vegetables are tender. Stir in flour until smooth. Gradually add broth; bring to a boil, stirring constantly.

Reduce heat to low; slowly add sour cream. Cook and stir until smooth. Stir in cream and milk. Add lemon juice, hot pepper sauce, salt and pepper. Heat through but do not boil. **Yield:** 6 servings.

chunky beef noodle soup

Lil Morris, Emerald Park, Saskatchewan
My husband and I lived for 11 years in the Arctic, where there was very little fresh produce and I had to order nonperishable groceries for a year ahead of time. This hearty soup—a meal in itself served with warm rolls— became a staple in our diet because it requires ingredients I could easily find.

- 1 **pound boneless round steak, cut into 1/2-inch cubes**
- 1 **medium onion, chopped**
- 2 **garlic cloves, minced**
- 1 **tablespoon vegetable oil**
- 2 **cups water**
- 1 **can (14-1/2 ounces) diced tomatoes, undrained**
- 1 **can (10-1/2 ounces) condensed beef consomme, undiluted**
- 1 to 2 **teaspoons chili powder**
- 1 **teaspoon salt**
- 1/2 **teaspoon dried oregano**
- 1 **cup uncooked spiral pasta**
- 1 **medium green pepper, chopped**
- 1/4 **cup minced fresh parsley**

In a large saucepan, cook round steak, onion and garlic in oil until the meat is browned and the onion is tender, about 5 minutes. Stir in water, tomatoes, consomme and seasonings; bring to a boil.

Reduce heat; cover and simmer until meat is tender, about 1-1/2 hours. Stir in pasta and green pepper. Simmer, uncovered, until noodles are tender, about 8 minutes. Add parsley. **Yield:** 8 servings (2 quarts).

swedish meatball soup

Debora Taylor, Inkom, Idaho
*To me, this is a very comforting, filling, homey soup.
I especially like cooking it during winter months and
serving it with hot rolls, bread or muffins.*

    1 egg
    2 cups half-and-half cream, *divided*
    1 cup soft bread crumbs
    1 small onion, finely chopped
1-3/4 teaspoons salt, *divided*
1-1/2 pounds ground beef
    1 tablespoon butter
    3 tablespoons all-purpose flour
  3/4 teaspoon beef bouillon granules
  1/2 teaspoon pepper
  1/8 to 1/4 teaspoon garlic salt
    3 cups water
    1 pound red potatoes, cubed
    1 package (10 ounces) frozen peas, thawed

In a bowl, beat egg; add 1/3 cup cream, bread crumbs,
onion and 1 teaspoon of salt. Add beef; mix well. Shape
into 1/2-in. balls. In a Dutch oven or soup kettle, brown
meatballs in butter, half at a time. Remove from the pan;
set aside. Drain fat.

To pan, add flour, bouillon, pepper, garlic salt and
remaining salt; stir until smooth. Gradually stir in
water; bring to a boil, stirring often. Add potatoes and
meatballs.

Reduce heat; cover and simmer for 25 minutes or until
the potatoes are tender. Stir in the peas and remaining
cream; heat through. **Yield:** 9 servings (about 2 quarts).

stir-fried pork soup

Louise Johnson, Harriman, Tennessee
*Especially to guests who enjoy the variety of Chinese
cooking, this is a treat. I like serving it with fried
noodles or rice as a side dish.*

2/3 pound boneless pork loin, cut into thin strips
    1 cup sliced fresh mushrooms
    1 cup chopped celery
  1/2 cup diced carrots
    2 tablespoons vegetable oil
    6 cups chicken broth
  1/2 cup chopped fresh spinach
    2 tablespoons cornstarch
    3 tablespoons cold water
    1 egg, lightly beaten
Pepper to taste

In a 3-qt. saucepan, stir-fry pork, mushrooms, celery and
carrots in oil until pork is no longer pink and vegetables
are tender. Add broth and spinach. Combine cornstarch
and water to make a thin paste; stir into soup. Return to
a boil; boil for 1 minute. Quickly stir in egg. Add
pepper. Serve immediately. **Yield:** 4-6 servings.

---

*To make a creamy potato soup extra
special, top it with crumbled cooked
bacon, shredded cheese and/or
herbed croutons.

Kelly Parsons, Seale, Alabama

---

cream of cabbage soup

Helen Riesterer, Kiel, Wisconsin

I've given this soup recipe to friends, who have varied it a little. One substituted summer squash and zucchini for the rutabaga. She said it tasted just great that way, too.

- 4 cups water
- 2 tablespoons chicken bouillon granules
- 3 cups diced peeled potatoes
- 1 cup finely chopped onion
- 1 cup diced peeled rutabaga
- 1/2 cup diced carrots
- 6 cups chopped cabbage
- 1 cup chopped celery
- 1/2 cup chopped green pepper
- 1 garlic clove, minced
- 1 teaspoon salt
- 1 teaspoon dill weed
- 1 cup butter
- 1 cup all-purpose flour
- 2 cups milk
- 2 cups chicken broth
- 1/2 pound process cheese (Velveeta), cubed
- 1/2 teaspoon dried thyme

Pepper to taste
Additional milk, optional

In a Dutch oven or soup kettle, bring water and bouillon to a boil. Add potatoes, onion, rutabaga and carrots. Reduce heat; cover and simmer for 5 minutes. Add cabbage, celery and green pepper; simmer, uncovered, for 5 minutes or until vegetables are crisp-tender. Add garlic, salt and dill.

In a saucepan, melt butter. Stir in flour; cook and stir over medium heat until golden. Gradually add milk and broth, stirring until smooth. Add cheese, thyme and pepper; cook on low until cheese is melted. Stir into vegetable mixture; simmer for 5 minutes. Thin with milk if needed. **Yield:** 12-14 servings (about 3-1/2 quarts).

monterey jack cheese soup

Susan Salenski, Copemish, Michigan

Main-meal soups are something I'm always on the lookout for. Since I love cheese and our kids like anything with Mexican flavor, I knew this one would be popular at our house. I've served it with tacos, nachos or a loaf of bread.

- 1 cup chicken broth
- 1 large tomato, peeled, seeded and diced
- 1/2 cup finely chopped onion
- 2 tablespoons chopped green chilies
- 1 garlic clove, minced
- 2 tablespoons butter
- 2 tablespoons all-purpose flour

Salt and pepper to taste
- 3 cups milk, *divided*
- 1-1/2 cups (6 ounces) shredded Monterey Jack cheese

In a 3-qt. saucepan, combine the first five ingredients; bring to a boil. Reduce heat; cover and simmer for 10 minutes or until vegetables are tender. Remove from the heat and set aside.

In another saucepan, melt butter. Stir in flour, salt and pepper. Cook and stir over medium heat until smooth. Gradually stir in 1-1/2 cups milk; bring to a boil. Boil for 1 minute, stirring constantly. Slowly stir into vegetable mixture. Add cheese and remaining milk. Cook and stir over low heat until cheese is melted. Serve immediately. **Yield:** 5 servings.

chicken 'n' dumpling soup

Rachel Hinz, St. James, Minnesota

This recipe's one I had to learn to marry into my husband's family! It is the traditional Hinz Christmas Eve meal, served before going to church. My father was a pastor who was always too keyed up from preaching to enjoy a big Sunday dinner. So I learned to make soup early on.

- 1 broiler/fryer chicken (3 to 3-1/2 pounds)
- 3 quarts water
- 1/4 cup chicken bouillon granules
- 1 bay leaf
- 1 teaspoon whole peppercorns
- 1/8 teaspoon ground allspice
- 6 cups uncooked wide noodles
- 4 cups sliced carrots
- 1 package (10 ounces) frozen mixed vegetables
- 3/4 cup sliced celery
- 1/2 cup chopped onion
- 1/4 cup uncooked long grain rice
- 2 tablespoons minced fresh parsley

DUMPLINGS:
- 1-1/3 cups all-purpose flour
- 2 teaspoons baking powder
- 1 teaspoon dried thyme
- 1/2 teaspoon salt
- 2/3 cup milk
- 2 tablespoons vegetable oil

In a Dutch oven or soup kettle, combine the first six ingredients; bring to a boil. Reduce heat; cover and simmer for 1-1/2 hours. Remove chicken; allow to cool. Strain broth; discard bay leaf and peppercorns. Skim fat. Debone chicken and cut into chunks; return chicken and broth to pan. Add noodles, vegetables, rice and parsley; bring to a simmer.

For dumplings, combine flour, baking powder, thyme and salt in a bowl. Combine milk and oil; stir into dry ingredients. Drop by teaspoonfuls onto simmering soup. Reduce heat; cover and simmer for 15 minutes (do not lift the cover). **Yield:** 20 servings (5 quarts).

prize winning tips

* I make and freeze several batches of basic chicken soup in two-serving and four-serving containers. Then for a quick supper, I simply reheat the soup, add rice or pasta and cook for 20 to 30 minutes.

Coral Smith, Mt. Ayr, Iowa

* Homemade tomato soup provides a wonderful base for spaghetti or vegetable soup, as well as a tasty addition to meat loaf.

Juanita Pardue, Heath Springs, South Carolina

* Crushed red pepper flakes add extra zing to minestrone soup.

Nancy Solberg, Madison, Wisconsin

best chicken noodle soup

Cheryl Rogers, Ames, Iowa

For years, I worked at making a chicken soup that tasted just like my mother's. When I realized I couldn't, I decided to come up with my own recipe. It was an immediate hit!

- 1 tablespoon dried rosemary, crushed
- 2 teaspoons garlic powder
- 2 teaspoons pepper
- 2 teaspoons seasoned salt
- 2 broiler/fryer chickens (3 to 3-1/2 pounds *each*)
- 1-1/2 quarts chicken broth
- 2-1/4 cups sliced fresh mushrooms
- 1/2 cup *each* chopped celery and onion
- 1/2 cup sliced carrots
- 1/4 teaspoon pepper

NOODLES:
- 2-1/2 cups all-purpose flour, *divided*
- 1 teaspoon salt
- 2 eggs
- 1 can (5 ounces) evaporated milk
- 1 tablespoon olive oil

Combine first four ingredients; rub over chickens. Place in an ungreased 13-in. x 9-in. x 2-in. baking pan. Cover and bake at 350° for 1-1/4 hours or until tender. Drain and reserve drippings. Skim fat. Cool chicken; debone and cut into chunks. Cover and refrigerate chicken.

In a Dutch oven or soup kettle, bring chicken broth and reserved drippings to a boil. Add mushrooms, celery, onion, carrots and pepper; simmer for 30 minutes.

Meanwhile, for noodles, set aside 1/3 cup of flour. Combine salt and remaining flour in a bowl. Beat eggs, milk and oil; stir into the dry ingredients. Sprinkle kneading surface with reserved flour; knead dough until smooth. Divide into thirds. Roll out each portion to 1/8-in. thickness; cut to desired width.

Freeze two portions to use at another time. Bring soup to a boil. Add one portion of noodles; cook for 7-9 minutes or until almost tender. Add chicken; heat through. **Yield:** 10 servings (2-3/4 quarts).

lentil barley soup

Anita Warner, Mt. Crawford, Virginia

Soups are one of my favorite things to prepare—they're so easy, and nothing is better on a chilly evening with some homemade bread or biscuits. I don't consider myself an "experienced" cook, but I do love to try new recipes with a country flair.

- 1 medium onion, chopped
- 1/2 cup chopped green pepper
- 3 garlic cloves, minced
- 1 tablespoon butter
- 1 can (49-1/2 ounces) chicken broth
- 3 medium carrots, chopped
- 1/2 cup dry lentils
- 1-1/2 teaspoons Italian seasoning
- 1 teaspoon salt
- 1/4 teaspoon pepper
- 1 cup cubed cooked chicken *or* turkey
- 1/2 cup quick-cooking barley
- 2 medium fresh mushrooms, chopped
- 1 can (28 ounces) crushed tomatoes, undrained

In a Dutch oven or soup kettle, saute the onion, green pepper and garlic in butter until tender. Add the broth, carrots, lentils, Italian seasoning, salt and pepper; bring to a boil. Reduce heat; cover and simmer for 25 minutes.

Add the chicken, barley and mushrooms; return to a boil. Reduce heat; cover and simmer for 10-15 minutes or until the lentils, barley and carrots are tender. Add the tomatoes and heat through. **Yield:** 8-10 servings (about 2-1/2 quarts).

savory tomato beef soup

Edna Tilley, Morganton, North Carolina
This soup's one my mother taught me to make. It's good all year but especially when the weather's cold. In winter, I serve it with grilled cheese sandwiches. It would also be a nice lunch with a side salad or homemade corn bread. Even our grandchildren—we have four—like it. It's a good way of getting them to eat their vegetables.

- 1 **pound beef stew meat, cut into 1/2-inch cubes**
- 1 **small meaty beef soup bone**
- 2 **tablespoons vegetable oil**
- 4 **cups water**
- 1 **can (28 ounces) diced tomatoes, undrained**
- 1 **cup chopped carrots**
- 1 **cup chopped celery**
- 1/4 **cup chopped celery leaves**
- 1 **tablespoon salt**
- 1/2 **teaspoon dried marjoram**
- 1/2 **teaspoon dried basil**
- 1/4 **teaspoon dried savory**
- 1/4 **teaspoon dried thyme**
- 1/8 **teaspoon ground mace**
- 1/8 **teaspoon hot pepper sauce**

In a Dutch oven or soup kettle, brown the stew meat and soup bone in oil. Add the remaining ingredients; bring to a boil. Reduce heat; cover and simmer for 4-5 hours or until meat is tender.

Skim fat. Remove meat from bone; cut into 1/2-in. cubes. Return to the soup and heat through. **Yield:** 6-8 servings (about 2 quarts).

split pea sausage soup

Donna Mae Young, Menomonie, Wisconsin
When my husband and I eat out and enjoy a dish, I go home and try to duplicate it. That's how I came up with this recipe. While it's good at any time, we like it full and hearty over the winter.

- 1 **pound smoked kielbasa**
- 1 **pound dried split peas**
- 6 **cups water**
- 1 **cup chopped carrots**
- 1 **cup chopped onion**
- 1 **cup chopped celery**
- 1 **tablespoon minced fresh parsley**
- 1 **teaspoon salt**
- 1/2 **teaspoon coarse black pepper**
- 2 **bay leaves**

Cut sausage in half lengthwise; cut into 1/4-in. pieces. Place in a Dutch oven or soup kettle; add remaining ingredients. Bring to a boil.

Reduce heat; cover and simmer for 1-1/4 to 1-1/2 hours or until peas are tender. Remove bay leaves. **Yield:** 8 servings (2 quarts).

> *The night before I prepare a big kettle of soup, I chop and measure all the veggies and refrigerate them in resealable plastic bags or in covered bowls. Next day, assembling the soup is a breeze!
> Rose Boudreaux, Bourg, Louisiana

SATISFYING SANDWICHES

#1

GRILLED HAM
AND EGG SALAD
SANDWICHES

grilled ham and egg salad sandwiches
GRAND PRIZE WINNER

You'll never settle for the same old sandwiches after seeing the dozen award-winning recipes from our Satisfying Sandwiches contest! These hearty handfuls will likely get you "on a roll" fixing new favorites for lunch-on-the-go or a casual supper.

"The hearty ham and toasted bread make it a deliciously different kind of egg salad sandwich."

The top picks from more than 2,000 entries include delectable fillings of beef, chicken and turkey, salmon and tuna, ham, eggs, sausage and a variety of vegetables. Some are served hot; some cold.

When it came down to the last savory bite, our tasting panel gave the Grand Prize to Beverly Stiger of Wolf Creek, Montana for her Grilled Ham and Egg Salad Sandwiches.

"An aunt shared this wonderful recipe with me years ago when I was looking for some low-budget meals," says Beverly. "The hearty ham and toasted bread make it a deliciously different kind of egg salad sandwich."

    6 hard-cooked eggs, chopped
    1 cup diced fully cooked ham
    1/2 cup finely chopped celery
    1 tablespoon minced onion
    1/2 cup mayonnaise
    2 teaspoons prepared mustard
    1/2 teaspoon salt
    1/4 teaspoon pepper
    12 slices whole wheat *or* white bread
Vegetable oil
BATTER:
    1/2 cup cornmeal
    1/2 cup all-purpose flour
    1 teaspoon baking powder
    1 teaspoon salt
    2 cups milk
    2 eggs, lightly beaten

Combine eggs, ham, celery, onion, mayonnaise, mustard, salt and pepper; spread on six slices of bread. Top with remaining bread and set aside.

In a bowl, whisk batter ingredients until well blended. Heat about 1/2 in. of oil in a large deep skillet. Dip sandwiches into batter. Fry in hot oil for 3 minutes on each side or until golden brown. Drain on paper towels. **Yield:** 6 servings.

french dip

Margaret McNeil, Memphis, Tennessee

For a sandwich with more pizzazz than the traditional French dip, give this recipe a try. The seasonings give the broth a wonderful flavor, and the meat cooks up tender and juicy. As an added bonus, the meat cooks in the slow cooker all day, so there's little fuss to making them. I promise that this new version will soon be a favorite at your house, too.

  1 beef chuck roast (3 pounds), trimmed
  2 cups water
1/2 cup soy sauce
  1 teaspoon dried rosemary
  1 teaspoon dried thyme
  1 teaspoon garlic powder
  1 bay leaf
  3 to 4 whole peppercorns
  8 French rolls, split

Place roast in a slow cooker. Add water, soy sauce and seasonings. Cover and cook on high for 5-6 hours or until beef is tender.

Remove the meat from the broth; shred with forks and keep warm. Strain broth and skim off fat. Pour broth into small cups for dipping. Serve beef on rolls. **Yield:** 8 servings.

salmon salad sandwiches

Yvonne Shust, Shoal Lake, Manitoba

These are perfect to pack in your kids' insulated lunch boxes when they can't face another boring peanut butter and jelly sandwich. Adults love them as well! We think the salmon, cream cheese and dill tucked inside a crusty wheat bun is simply delicious. The carrots and celery add a nice crunch.

  1 package (3 ounces) cream cheese, softened
  1 tablespoon mayonnaise
  1 tablespoon lemon juice
  1 teaspoon dill weed
1/4 to 1/2 teaspoon salt
1/8 teaspoon pepper
  1 can (6 ounces) pink salmon, drained, skin and bones removed
1/2 cup shredded carrot
1/2 cup chopped celery
Lettuce leaves
  2 whole wheat buns, split

In a mixing bowl, beat cream cheese, mayonnaise, lemon juice, dill, salt and pepper until smooth. Add the salmon, carrot and celery and mix well. Place a lettuce leaf and about 1/2 cup salmon salad on each bun. **Yield:** 2 servings.

baked southwest sandwiches

Holly Sorensen, Reedley, California
I like to prepare these tasty sandwiches whenever I have a few friends over for an informal lunch. The combination of toppings is out of this world. I'm often asked for the recipe.

- 1 can (4-1/4 ounces) chopped ripe olives, drained
- 1/2 teaspoon chili powder
- 1/2 teaspoon ground cumin
- 1/4 teaspoon salt
- 1/2 cup mayonnaise
- 1/3 cup sour cream
- 1/3 cup chopped green onions
- 8 slices Italian bread
- 3/4 to 1 pound thinly sliced cooked turkey
- 2 medium tomatoes, thinly sliced
- 2 ripe avocados, sliced
- 3/4 cup shredded cheddar cheese
- 3/4 cup shredded Monterey Jack cheese

In a bowl, combine olives, chili powder, cumin and salt; set aside 2 tablespoons. Add the mayonnaise, sour cream and onions to the remaining olive mixture.

Place bread on an ungreased baking sheet; spread 1 tablespoon of mayonnaise mixture on each slice. Top with the turkey and tomatoes. Spread with another tablespoon of mayonnaise mixture; top with avocados and cheeses. Sprinkle with reserved olive mixture. Bake at 350° for 15 minutes or until heated through. **Yield:** 8 servings.

italian sloppy joes

Kimberly Speakman, McKinney, Texas
My mother used to make these filling sandwiches for us when we were kids. When I grew up and left home, I was sure to take the recipe with me, and now it's one of my husband's favorite dinners. The meat mixture tastes somewhat like pizza. They're a nice change of pace from the more traditional sloppy joes.

- 1 pound bulk Italian sausage
- 1 pound bulk hot Italian sausage
- 4 garlic cloves, minced
- 1 cup chopped green pepper
- 1/2 cup chopped onion
- 1 can (15 ounces) tomato sauce
- 2 tablespoons minced fresh parsley
- 1 teaspoon dried oregano
- 1/2 teaspoon chili powder
- 1/4 teaspoon fennel seed
- 8 to 10 French *or* submarine rolls, split
- 3/4 cup shredded mozzarella cheese

In a large saucepan or Dutch oven over medium heat, cook sausage, garlic, green pepper and onion until the sausage is no longer pink; drain.

Add the tomato sauce and seasonings; bring to a boil. Reduce heat; cover and simmer for 30 minutes. Spoon about 1/2 cup onto each roll; sprinkle with cheese. **Yield:** 8-10 servings.

dilly turkey melt

Henry Mujica, North Riverside, Illinois

This is a hearty grilled sandwich with a distinctive and delicious combination of ingredients, like turkey, Canadian bacon and Monterey Jack cheese. The dill pickle slices add a bit of fun, and the barbecue sauce provides a hint of sweetness that's irresistible. They're delicious served alongside a steaming bowl of soup for a satisfying lunch or supper.

- 2 medium onions, sliced
- 4 tablespoons butter, *divided*
- 4 tablespoons barbecue sauce
- 8 slices sourdough bread
- 8 slices Monterey Jack cheese
- 8 slices Canadian bacon
- 8 slices cooked turkey

Dill pickle slices

In a large skillet, saute the onions in 1 tablespoon of butter until tender; remove and set aside. Spread the barbecue sauce on four slices of the bread. Layer each with one slice of cheese, bacon, turkey, pickles, onions and another slice of cheese. Cover with remaining slices of bread.

In the same skillet over medium-low heat, melt remaining butter. Cook sandwiches on both sides until golden brown and cheese is melted (skillet may be covered the last few minutes to help melt cheese if necessary). **Yield:** 4 servings.

nutty chicken pita sandwiches

Glenda Schwarz, Morden, Manitoba

When company is coming for lunch, this is my favorite sandwich to make, since it looks and tastes a bit fancy. Even kids like it because of the crunchy nuts and creamy filling inside the pita bread halves.

- 1 package (8 ounces) cream cheese, softened
- 3 tablespoons milk
- 1 tablespoon lemon juice
- 2 cups cubed cooked chicken
- 1/2 cup chopped green pepper
- 2 tablespoons chopped green onions
- 1 teaspoon ground mustard
- 1/2 teaspoon dried thyme
- 1/2 teaspoon salt
- 1/8 teaspoon pepper
- 1/4 cup chopped walnuts
- 3 large pita breads, halved

Alfalfa sprouts, optional

In a mixing bowl, beat the cream cheese, milk and lemon juice until smooth. Stir in the chicken, green pepper, onions, mustard, thyme, salt and pepper; refrigerate until serving.

Just before serving, stir in the walnuts. Spoon about 1/2 cup filling into each pita half. Top with alfalfa sprouts if desired. **Yield:** 3-6 servings.

sausage-stuffed loaf

Mary Koehler, Portland, Oregon

I love to serve this hearty sandwich of sausage and ground beef in a zesty spaghetti sauce stuffed inside of a loaf of French bread. Topped with melted cheese, it's a real crowd-pleaser every time.

- 2 Italian sausages
- 1/2 pound ground beef
- 1/2 cup chopped onion
- 1/4 cup chopped green pepper
- 1 medium tomato, chopped
- 1 can (15 ounces) chunky Italian-style tomato sauce
- 1/2 teaspoon dried basil
- 1/2 teaspoon dried oregano
- 1/2 teaspoon sugar
- 1/4 teaspoon aniseed
- 1/4 teaspoon salt
- 1/8 teaspoon garlic powder
- 1 loaf (1 pound) French bread
- 1/4 to 1/2 cup shredded Parmesan cheese

Coarsely ground pepper

In a skillet, cook sausages until no longer pink. Remove and set aside. In the same skillet, cook beef, onion and green pepper until beef is no longer pink; drain. Stir in tomato, tomato sauce and seasonings.

Cut sausages in half lengthwise and slice; add to meat sauce. Cut a wedge out of top of the bread, about 2 in. wide and three-fourths of the way through the loaf. Fill loaf with meat sauce. Sprinkle with Parmesan cheese and pepper. Wrap in heavy-duty foil. Bake at 400° for 15-20 minutes or until heated through. **Yield:** 6 servings.

prize winning tips

* * * * *

* Here's what I do when I need chopped hard-cooked eggs for egg salad. Instead of boiling the eggs, I poach them until the egg yolks are cooked through. They're done in a matter of minutes and don't have to be peeled before chopping...just drain and pat dry. This method saves about 20 to 30 minutes!

Judy Thouvenel, Aledo, Texas

* For a speedy sandwich, slice a croissant in half and warm in the microwave. Spread the halves with a little mustard, then add a slice of Virginia ham, roast beef and Swiss cheese. Top it off with leaf lettuce and serve it with cherry tomatoes.

Malvine Pataki Esposito, Myrtle Beach, South Carolina

* When I have a big slice of meat loaf in the refrigerator, I chop it up and add mayonnaise and diced onion to taste. Spread on a bun or bread, it makes a delicious sandwich.

Penny Bray, Williamsport, Indiana

barbecued hot dogs

Joyce Koehler, Watertown, Wisconsin

I grew up in a family of eight kids, and we never complained if Mom made these terrific hot dogs often for birthday parties and other family gatherings. You'll find that kids and grown-ups devour these... good thing they're easy to make. The from-scratch barbecue sauce you serve with them is superb!

- 3/4 cup chopped onion
- 3 tablespoons butter
- 1-1/2 cups chopped celery
- 1-1/2 cups ketchup
- 3/4 cup water
- 1/3 cup lemon juice
- 3 tablespoons brown sugar
- 3 tablespoons vinegar
- 1 tablespoon Worcestershire sauce
- 1 tablespoon yellow mustard
- 2 packages (1 pound *each*) hot dogs
- 20 hot dog buns, split

In a saucepan over medium heat, saute the onion in butter until tender. Add the celery, ketchup, water, lemon juice, sugar, vinegar, Worcestershire sauce and mustard; bring to a boil. Reduce heat; cover and simmer for 30 minutes.

Cut three 1/4-in.-deep slits on each side of hot the dogs; place in a 2-1/2-qt. baking dish. Pour the barbecue sauce over the hot dogs. Cover and bake at 350° for 40-45 minutes or until heated through. Serve on buns. **Yield:** 20 servings.

tuna burgers

Nancy Selig, Lunenburg, Nova Scotia

I gave Mom's original recipe a boost by adding onion and green pepper to these delightfully different tuna sandwiches. With hard-cooked eggs and cheese, the filling tastes fresh, not fishy, and the rolls stay nice and crispy. Try them the next time you have a taste for tuna but with a twist.

- 6 hard-cooked eggs, chopped
- 2 cans (6 ounces *each*) tuna, drained and flaked
- 1 cup (4 ounces) shredded sharp cheddar cheese
- 1/2 cup chopped green pepper
- 1/2 cup chopped onion
- 3/4 teaspoon garlic salt
- 3/4 teaspoon pepper
- 1 cup mayonnaise
- 8 kaiser rolls, split

In a bowl, combine eggs and tuna. Add the cheese, green pepper, onion, garlic salt and pepper; mix well. Stir in the mayonnaise.

Spoon about 1/2 cup onto each roll; wrap individually in heavy-duty foil. Bake at 400° for 15 minutes or until heated through. **Yield:** 8 servings.

runners-up

hearty chicken club

Debbie Johanesen, Missoula, Montana
I discovered the recipe for this sizable sandwich a while back and modified it to suit my family's tastes. We love it…the only problem is trying to open wide enough to take a bite!

- 1/4 **cup mayonnaise**
- 2 **tablespoons salsa**
- 4 **slices seven-grain sandwich bread**
- 2 **lettuce leaves**
- 4 **slices tomato**
- 8 **ounces sliced cooked chicken *or* turkey**
- 4 **bacon strips, cooked**
- 4 **slices cheddar cheese**
- 1 **ripe avocado, sliced**

Combine mayonnaise and salsa; spread on two slices of bread. Layer with lettuce, tomato, chicken or turkey, bacon, cheese and avocado. Top with remaining bread. **Yield:** 2 servings.

✱To give hot dogs extra flavor without a lot of effort, first pierce them a few times with a fork. Then marinate them in Worcestershire sauce for 30 minutes before grilling. I often stir a little garlic and onion powder into the sauce, too.
Stephen Hill, Reading, Pennsylvania

---

big sandwich

Margaret Yost, Tipp City, Ohio
One look at this sandwich and your family will know they're in for a treat. People always ask how they're supposed to eat it. I tell them to dig in and enjoy!

- 1 **unsliced round loaf of bread (8 inches)**
- 2 **tablespoons horseradish**
- 1/2 **pound thinly sliced cooked roast beef**
- 2 **tablespoons prepared mustard**
- 1/2 **pound thinly sliced fully cooked ham**
  ***or* turkey**
- 4 **slices Swiss cheese**
- 2 **tablespoons mayonnaise**
- 1 **small tomato, thinly sliced**
- 6 **bacon strips, cooked**
- 4 **slices American cheese**
- 1 **small onion, thinly sliced**
- 1/4 **cup butter, melted**
- 1 **tablespoon sesame seeds**
- 1/2 **teaspoon onion salt**

Slice bread horizontally into five equal layers. Spread bottom layer with horseradish; top with roast beef. Place the next slice of bread over beef; spread with mustard and top with ham or turkey and Swiss cheese. Add the next slice of bread; spread with mayonnaise and top with tomato and bacon. Add the next slice of bread; top with American cheese and onion. Cover with remaining bread.

Combine butter, sesame seeds and onion salt; brush over top and sides of loaf. Place on a baking sheet; loosely tent with heavy-duty foil. Bake at 400° for 15-20 minutes or until heated through. Carefully slice into eight wedges. **Yield:** 8 servings.

"SAY CHEESE!"

#1

SAVORY
CHEESE SOUP

savory cheese soup

Cheese has a wonderful way of making everything you cook taste better. It adds appeal to cooked vegetables, builds creamy richness into snacks, soups and desserts, brings tang to dressings and sauces and makes hearty main dishes even more satisfying.

> "Its big cheese flavor blends wonderfully with the flavor of the vegetables."

Our "Say Cheese!" contest proved the popularity of this "dairy" good ingredient—cooks from across the country entered nearly 3,000 recipes featuring many of their favorite cheeses like flavorful cheddar, mozzarella, Parmesan and Swiss.

The 12 cheesy choices our judges selected as the winners are sure to bring satisfied smiles to the faces of family and friends when you prepare the recipes in your kitchen, too. Grand Prize Winner Savory Cheese Soup especially so.

"This delicious soup recipe was shared by a friend and instantly became a hit with my husband," says Dee Falk of Stromsburg, Nebraska. "Its big cheese flavor blends wonderfully with the flavor of the vegetables."

1/4 cup chopped onion
3 tablespoons butter
1/4 cup all-purpose flour
1/4 teaspoon salt
1/8 teaspoon pepper
1/8 teaspoon garlic powder
2 cups milk
1 can (14-1/2 ounces) chicken broth
1/2 cup shredded carrots
1/2 cup finely chopped celery
1-1/2 cups (6 ounces) shredded cheddar cheese
3/4 cup shredded mozzarella cheese
Fresh *or* dried chives, optional

In a large saucepan, saute onion in butter until tender. Add flour, salt, pepper and garlic powder; stir until smooth. Gradually add milk; cook and stir over medium heat until thickened and bubbly.

Meanwhile, bring chicken broth to a boil in a small saucepan. Add carrots and celery; simmer for 5 minutes or until vegetables are tender. Add to milk mixture and stir until blended. Add cheeses. Cook and stir until melted (do not boil). Garnish with chives if desired. **Yield:** about 4 servings.

muenster bread

Melanie Mero, Ida, Michigan

My sister and I won blue ribbons in 4-H with this bread many years ago. The recipe makes a beautiful round loaf with a layer of cheese peeking out of every slice.

- 2 packages (1/4 ounce *each*) active dry yeast
- 1 cup warm milk (110° to 115°)
- 1/2 cup butter, softened
- 2 tablespoons sugar
- 1 teaspoon salt
- 3-1/4 to 3-3/4 cups all-purpose flour
- 1 egg plus 1 egg yolk
- 4 cups (1 pound) shredded Muenster cheese
- 1 egg white, beaten

In a large mixing bowl, dissolve yeast in milk. Add butter, sugar, salt and 2 cups flour; beat until smooth. Stir in enough remaining flour to form a soft dough.

Turn onto a floured surface; knead until smooth and elastic, about 6-8 minutes. Place in a greased bowl, turning once to grease top. Cover and let rise in a warm place until doubled, about 1 hour. In a large bowl, beat egg and yolk; stir in cheese.

Punch dough down; roll into a 16-in. circle. Place in a greased 9-in. round baking pan, letting dough drape over the edges. Spoon the cheese mixture into center of dough. Gather dough up over filling in 1-1/2-in. pleats. Gently squeeze pleats together at top and twist to make a top knot. Allow to rise 10-15 minutes.

Brush loaf with egg white. Bake at 375° for 45-50 minutes. Cool on a wire rack for 20 minutes. Serve warm. **Yield:** 1 loaf.

cheese-stuffed shells

Lori Mecca, Grants Pass, Oregon

I tasted this rich cheesy pasta dish at an Italian restaurant. I got the recipe and made a few changes to it.

- 1 pound bulk Italian sausage
- 1 large onion, chopped
- 1 package (10 ounces) frozen chopped spinach, cooked and well drained
- 1 package (8 ounces) cream cheese, softened
- 1 egg, beaten
- 2 cups (8 ounces) shredded mozzarella cheese, *divided*
- 2 cups (8 ounces) shredded cheddar cheese
- 1 cup cottage cheese
- 1/4 cup grated Parmesan cheese
- 1/4 teaspoon *each* salt and pepper
- 1/8 teaspoon ground cinnamon, optional
- 20 jumbo shell noodles, cooked and drained

SAUCE:
- 1 can (29 ounces) tomato sauce
- 1 tablespoon dried minced onion
- 1-1/2 teaspoons *each* dried basil and parsley flakes
- 2 garlic cloves, minced
- 1 teaspoon *each* sugar and dried oregano
- 1/2 teaspoon salt
- 1/4 teaspoon pepper

In a skillet, cook sausage and onion until meat is no longer pink; drain. Transfer to a large bowl. Stir in spinach, cream cheese and egg. Add 1 cup mozzarella, cheddar, cottage cheese, Parmesan and seasonings; mix well.

Stuff shells and arrange in a greased 13-in. x 9-in. x 2-in. baking dish. Combine sauce ingredients. Spoon over shells. Cover and bake at 350° for 40 minutes. Uncover; sprinkle with remaining mozzarella. Return to oven for 5 minutes or until cheese melts. **Yield:** 8-10 servings.

mozzarella sticks

Mary Merchant, Barre, Vermont
I'm particularly fond of these tasty snacks because they're baked, not fried. Cheese is one of my family's favorite foods. Being of Italian descent, I cook often with ricotta and mozzarella cheeses.

>   2 eggs
>   1 tablespoon water
>   1 cup dry bread crumbs
> 2-1/2 teaspoons Italian seasoning
>   1/2 teaspoon garlic powder
>   1/8 teaspoon pepper
>   12 sticks string cheese
>   3 tablespoons all-purpose flour
>   1 tablespoon butter, melted
>   1 cup marinara *or* spaghetti sauce, heated

In a small bowl, beat eggs and water. In a plastic bag, combine bread crumbs, Italian seasoning, garlic powder and pepper. Coat cheese sticks in flour, then dip in egg mixture and bread crumb mixture. Repeat egg and bread crumb coatings. Cover and chill for at least 4 hours or overnight.

Place on an ungreased baking sheet; drizzle with butter. Bake, uncovered, at 400° for 6-8 minutes or until heated through. Allow to stand for 3-5 minutes before serving. Use marinara or spaghetti sauce for dipping.
Yield: 4-6 servings.

Editor's Note: Regular mozzarella cheese, cut into 4-in. x 1/2-in. sticks, can be substituted for the string cheese.

blue cheese dressing

Barbara Nowakowski, North Tonawanda, New York
I tasted this tangy dressing for the first time at a friend's house. She gave me the recipe, and now I make it every week. I always keep some in my refrigerator. It tastes much better than bottled blue cheese dressing and is a snap to make.

> 1-1/2 cups mayonnaise
>   1/2 cup sour cream
>   1/4 cup cider vinegar
>   4 teaspoons sugar
>   1/2 teaspoon ground mustard
>   1/2 teaspoon garlic powder
>   1/2 teaspoon onion powder
>   1 package (4 ounces) blue cheese, crumbled

In a bowl, combine the first seven ingredients. Stir in the blue cheese. Cover and chill at least 2 hours. Store in the refrigerator. **Yield:** 2 cups.

> *My favorite leftover dish is lasagna soup. I just cut up leftover lasagna into small pieces and stir it into a can of tomato soup and the same amount of milk. After it's warm, I serve it with leftover garlic bread dressed up with mozzarella cheese.
>
> Bonnie Knight, Pewaukee, Wisconsin

hot pizza dip

Karen Riordan, Fern Creek, Kentucky

I'm a busy stay-at-home mom. I love this recipe because it's easy to prepare in advance and keep refrigerated. I simply put it in the oven when guests arrive, and by the time I've poured beverages, the dip is ready to serve. It gets gobbled up quickly!

- 1 package (8 ounces) cream cheese, softened
- 1 teaspoon Italian seasoning
- 1/4 teaspoon garlic powder
- 2 cups (8 ounces) shredded mozzarella cheese
- 1 cup (4 ounces) shredded cheddar cheese
- 1/2 cup pizza sauce
- 1/2 cup finely chopped green pepper
- 1/2 cup finely chopped sweet red pepper

Tortilla chips *or* breadsticks

In a bowl, combine the cream cheese, Italian seasoning and garlic powder; spread on the bottom of a greased 9-in. pie plate. Combine the mozzarella and cheddar cheeses; sprinkle half over the cream cheese layer. Top with the pizza sauce and peppers. Sprinkle with the remaining cheeses.

Bake at 350° for 20 minutes. Serve warm with tortilla chips or breadsticks. **Yield:** about 3-1/2 cups.

lasagna in a bun

Cindy Morelock, Afton, Tennessee

Here's an interesting and delicious way to serve a great main dish and enjoy several different cheeses. My family loves the meat sauce and cheese tucked into the buns.

- 8 sub *or* hoagie buns (8 inches)
- 1 pound ground beef
- 1 cup spaghetti sauce
- 1 tablespoon garlic powder
- 1 tablespoon dried Italian seasoning
- 1 cup ricotta cheese
- 1/4 cup grated Parmesan cheese
- 1 cup (4 ounces) shredded cheddar cheese, *divided*
- 1 cup (4 ounces) shredded mozzarella cheese, *divided*

Cut thin slices off the tops of the buns. Hollow out centers, leaving 1/4-in.-thick shells; discard tops and center or save for another use. In a skillet, cook ground beef over medium heat until no longer pink; drain. Add spaghetti sauce, garlic powder and Italian seasoning. Cook 4-5 minutes or until heated through.

Meanwhile, combine ricotta, Parmesan and half of cheddar and mozzarella cheeses; mix well. Spoon meat sauce into buns; top with cheese mixture. Place on a baking sheet. Cover loosely with foil.

Bake at 350° for 20-25 minutes. Uncover; sprinkle with remaining cheddar and mozzarella. Return to the oven for 2-3 minutes or until the cheese melts. **Yield:** 8 servings.

runners-up

luscious almond cheesecake

Brenda Clifford, Overland Park, Kansas

I received this recipe along with a set of springform pans from a cousin at my wedding shower. It makes a heavenly cheesecake. My son Tommy often requests it in place of a birthday cake.

CRUST:
1-1/4 cups crushed vanilla wafers
  3/4 cup finely chopped almonds
  1/4 cup sugar
  1/3 cup butter, melted

FILLING:
    4 packages (8 ounces *each*) cream cheese, softened
1-1/4 cups sugar
    4 eggs
1-1/2 teaspoons almond extract
    1 teaspoon vanilla extract

TOPPING:
    2 cups (16 ounces) sour cream
  1/4 cup sugar
    1 teaspoon vanilla extract
  1/8 cup toasted sliced almonds

In a bowl, combine wafers, almonds and sugar; add the butter and mix well. Press into the bottom of an ungreased 10-in. springform pan; set aside.

In a large mixing bowl, beat cream cheese and sugar until creamy. Add the eggs, one at a time, beating well after each addition. Add extracts; beat just until blended. Pour into crust. Bake at 350° for 55 minutes or until center is almost set. Remove from the oven; let stand for 5 minutes.

Combine sour cream, sugar and vanilla; spread over filling. Return to the oven for 5 minutes. Cool on a wire rack; chill overnight. Just before serving, sprinkle with almonds and remove sides of pan. Store in the refrigerator. **Yield:** 14-16 servings.

prize winning tips

✱For maximum flavor, I let platters of sliced cheese sit out at room temperature for 30 minutes before serving.

Beth Thompson, Spokane, Washington

✱My family loves cheese-stuffed manicotti, but stuffing the shells is no fun. A friend told me that she uses wonton wrappers instead of noodles. Simply place the filling on each wrapper and roll up. Then place the rolls in a pan seam side down and proceed with your regular recipe. After trying this method once, it is the only way I make manicotti.

Beverly Norris, Evanston, Wyoming

✱Cheese reacts quickly to heat, so it's best to cook it slowly over low heat. To prevent cheese from curdling when I'm making a sauce or fondue, I toss the shredded cheese with a little flour or cornstarch first.

Gale Narlock, Wausau, Wisconsin

runners-up

italian cheese twists

Marna Heitz, Farley, Iowa
My family loves breadsticks, and this recipe was an immediate success. The breadsticks look delicate and fancy, but they aren't tricky to make using prepared bread dough. We love the herb flavor.

- 1 loaf (1 pound) frozen bread dough, thawed
- 1/4 cup butter, softened
- 1/4 teaspoon garlic powder
- 1/4 teaspoon dried basil
- 1/4 teaspoon dried oregano
- 1/4 teaspoon dried marjoram
- 3/4 cup shredded mozzarella cheese
- 1 egg
- 1 tablespoon water
- 2 tablespoons sesame seeds *and/or* grated Parmesan cheese

On a lightly floured surface, roll dough into a 12-in. square. Combine butter and seasonings; spread over dough. Sprinkle with mozzarella cheese. Fold dough into thirds. Cut crosswise into 24 strips, 1/2 in. each. Twist each strip twice; pinch ends to seal.

Place 2 in. apart on a greased baking sheet. Cover and let rise in a warm place until almost doubled, about 30 minutes.

In a small bowl, beat egg and water; brush over the twists. Sprinkle with sesame seeds and/or Parmesan cheese. Bake at 375° for 10-12 minutes or until light golden brown. **Yield:** 2 dozen.

ranch mac 'n' cheese

Michelle Rotunno, Independence, Missouri
I came up with the recipe for this creamy and satisfying macaroni and cheese, which has a special twist. My husband requests it often—it's hearty enough to serve as a main dish.

- 1 cup milk
- 1/4 cup butter
- 2 envelopes ranch salad dressing mix
- 1 teaspoon lemon-pepper seasoning
- 1 teaspoon garlic pepper
- 1 teaspoon garlic salt
- 1 cup cubed Colby cheese
- 1 cup cubed Monterey Jack cheese
- 1 cup (8 ounces) sour cream
- 1/2 cup crushed saltines
- 1 pound elbow macaroni, cooked and drained
- Grated Parmesan cheese

In a Dutch oven, combine the first eight ingredients. Cook and stir over medium heat until cheese has melted and mixture begins to thicken.

Fold in the sour cream. Add crackers and macaroni. Cook until heated through, stirring frequently. Spoon into a serving dish; sprinkle with Parmesan cheese. **Yield:** 6-8 servings.

crustless swiss quiche

Marlene Kole, Highland Heights, Ohio
I received this recipe from my mother-in-law, an all-around great cook. Everyone raves about her rich quiche when she serves it at card parties. I love to cook, but I don't have a lot of time in the kitchen these days.

- 1/2 cup butter
- 1/2 cup all-purpose flour
- 1-1/2 cups milk
- 2-1/2 cups cottage cheese
- 1 teaspoon baking powder
- 1 teaspoon salt
- 1 teaspoon Dijon mustard
- 9 eggs
- 2 packages (one 8 ounces, one 3 ounces) cream cheese, softened
- 3 cups (12 ounces) shredded Swiss cheese
- 1/3 cup grated Parmesan cheese

Melt butter in a medium saucepan. Stir in flour; cook and stir until bubbly. Gradually add milk; cook over medium heat, stirring occasionally, until sauce thickens. Remove from the heat; set aside to cool, about 15-20 minutes.

Meanwhile, combine cottage cheese, baking powder, salt and mustard; set aside. In a large mixing bowl, beat the eggs. Slowly add cream cheese, cottage cheese mixture and cream sauce. Fold in Swiss and Parmesan cheeses.

Pour into two greased 10-in. pie plates. Bake at 350° for 40 minutes or until puffed and lightly browned. Serve immediately. **Yield:** 16-20 servings.

four-cheese lasagna

Janet Myers, Napanee, Ontario
Cheese really stars in this delicious lasagna, which I created a few years ago.

- 1 pound ground beef
- 1 medium onion, chopped
- 2 garlic cloves, minced
- 1 can (28 ounces) tomatoes, undrained
- 1 can (8 ounces) sliced mushrooms, drained
- 1 can (6 ounces) tomato paste
- 1 teaspoon salt
- 1 teaspoon *each* dried oregano and basil
- 1/2 teaspoon pepper
- 1/2 teaspoon fennel seed
- 1 carton (16 ounces) cottage cheese
- 2/3 cup grated Parmesan cheese
- 1/4 cup shredded mild cheddar cheese
- 1-1/2 cups (6 ounces) shredded mozzarella cheese, *divided*
- 2 eggs
- 1 pound lasagna noodles, cooked and drained

In a skillet, cook beef, onion and garlic over medium heat until beef is no longer pink and onion is tender; drain. In a blender, process the tomatoes until smooth. Stir into beef mixture along with mushrooms, tomato paste and seasonings; simmer 15 minutes. In a bowl, combine cottage cheese, Parmesan, cheddar, 1/2 cup mozzarella and eggs.

Spread 2 cups meat sauce in the bottom of an ungreased 13-in. x 9-in. x 2-in. baking dish. Arrange half the noodles over sauce. Spread cottage cheese mixture over noodles. Top with remaining noodles and meat sauce. Cover and bake at 350° for 45 minutes. Uncover; sprinkle with remaining mozzarella. Return to the oven for 15 minutes or until cheese melts. **Yield:** 12 servings.

SUPER SALADS

#1

ORANGE
AVOCADO SALAD

orange avocado salad

Summer meals taste so good when a satisfying salad is part of the menu. Garden-fresh mixtures look inviting on the table and really hit the spot when warmer weather calls for lighter fare.

For our Super Salads contest, salad-loving subscribers shared luscious leafy salads, colorful fruit combinations, tasty taco salads, pleasing pasta salads, marinated medleys of vegetables and more. We received 4,600 recipes in all!

"For a beautiful salad with an unbeatable combination of flavors, you can't miss with this recipe."

After much shredding, tossing and topping fresh ingredients with delightful dressings, our Test Kitchen staff presented our taste panel with salad bowls full of refreshing creations. Orange Avocado Salad, from Latressa Allen of Forth Worth, Texas, was selected as the Grand Prize Winner.

"For a beautiful salad with an unbeatable combination of flavors, you can't miss with this recipe," says Latressa. "We love the mellow avocado together with sweet mandarin oranges and crisp cucumber. The tangy dressing makes this dish special."

DRESSING:
- 1/2 cup orange juice
- 1/4 cup vegetable oil
- 2 tablespoons red wine vinegar
- 1 tablespoon sugar
- 1 teaspoon grated orange peel
- 1/4 teaspoon salt

SALAD:
- 1 medium head iceberg lettuce, torn
- 2 cups torn red leaf lettuce
- 1 medium ripe avocado, peeled and sliced
- 1/4 cup orange juice
- 1 cucumber, sliced
- 1/2 medium red onion, thinly sliced into rings
- 1 can (11 ounces) mandarin oranges, drained

In a jar with tight-fitting lid, combine dressing ingredients; shake well. Chill.

Just before serving, toss greens in a large salad bowl. Dip the avocado slices into orange juice; arrange over greens (discard remaining juice). Add cucumber, onion and oranges. Serve with dressing. **Yield:** 6-8 servings.

german cucumber salad

Julie Koren, Kennesaw, Georgia
This recipe came from a friend who ran his own inn in Germany. It's a very cool, light salad with an exhilarating taste that's delicious any time of the year—especially when made with fresh cucumbers and tomatoes.

- 2 medium cucumbers, thinly sliced
- 4 green onions, thinly sliced
- 3 small tomatoes, sliced
- 2 tablespoons snipped fresh parsley

DRESSING:
- 1/4 cup sour cream
- 1/4 teaspoon prepared mustard
- 2 tablespoons minced fresh dill
- 1 tablespoon vinegar
- 1 tablespoon milk
- 1/2 teaspoon salt
- 1/8 teaspoon pepper

In a bowl, combine cucumbers, onions, tomatoes and parsley. Combine dressing ingredients; pour over cucumber mixture and toss gently. Cover and chill for at least 1 hour. **Yield:** 4-6 servings.

> ***If you want the cucumbers in your salad to be cool and crunchy, just chill them overnight in ice water.**
> Ruby Williams, Bogalusa, Louisiana

mexican garden salad

Dianne Esposite, New Middletown, Ohio
I'm always watching for delicious new recipes to try, and when I found this salad, I knew it would taste as good as it looks. Although similar to a traditional taco salad, this recipe adds tasty extras like broccoli and carrot. It's stunning on the table.

- 1 pound ground beef
- 1 jar (16 ounces) thick and chunky salsa, *divided*
- 1/4 cup water
- 1 envelope taco seasoning mix
- 1-1/2 heads iceberg lettuce, torn
- 3 cups broccoli florets (about 1/2 pound)
- 1 small red onion, thinly sliced into rings
- 1 medium carrot, shredded
- 1 large tomato, chopped
- 1 can (4 ounces) chopped green chilies, drained
- 1/2 to 1 cup shredded cheddar cheese
- 1 cup (8 ounces) sour cream

Tortilla chips, optional

In a skillet, cook beef over medium heat until no longer pink; drain. Add 1 cup salsa, water and taco seasoning; bring to a boil. Reduce heat and simmer for 20 minutes; cool.

In a 3- or 4-qt. glass bowl, layer vegetables in order given. Top with the chilies, beef mixture and cheese. Combine sour cream and remaining salsa; serve with salad and tortilla chips if desired. **Yield:** 6-8 servings.

fruit salad supreme

Lois Rutherford, St. Augustine, Florida

For a delightful fruit salad that's a snap to prepare, give this recipe a try. The sweet combination of pineapple, orange and cantaloupe, topped with onion and a tangy lime dressing, is one family and friends ask for often. It's also one of my favorites to serve in place of the usual tossed green salad topped with croutons.

- 2 cups watercress, stems removed
- 8 fresh *or* canned pineapple rings, halved
- 2 oranges, peeled and sliced crosswise
- 1-1/2 cups cantaloupe chunks
- 1/4 cup sliced green onions *or* 1 small sweet onion, chopped

LIME DRESSING:

- 1/4 cup vegetable oil
- 2 tablespoons lime juice
- 1 tablespoon sugar
- 1/4 teaspoon hot pepper sauce
- 1 tablespoon sour cream

On individual salad plates, arrange the watercress, pineapple and oranges. Top with the cantaloupe and onions.

In a small bowl, whisk oil, lime juice, sugar and hot pepper sauce until sugar is dissolved. Stir in sour cream. Serve with salads. **Yield:** 4 servings.

minted melon salad

Terry Saylor, Vermillion, South Dakota

People can't resist digging into a salad made with colorful summer fruits. The unique dressing is what makes this salad a crowd-pleaser. I get compliments whenever I serve it, especially when I put it on the table in a melon boat. It's a warm-weather treat.

- 1 cup water
- 3/4 cup sugar
- 3 tablespoons lime juice
- 1-1/2 teaspoons chopped fresh mint
- 3/4 teaspoon aniseed

Pinch salt

- 5 cups cubed watermelon (about 1/2 medium melon)
- 3 cups cubed cantaloupe (about 1 medium melon)
- 3 cups cubed honeydew (about 1 medium melon)
- 2 cups peach slices (about 2 peaches)
- 1 cup fresh blueberries

In a small saucepan, bring the first six ingredients to a boil. Boil for 2 minutes; remove from the heat. Cover and cool syrup completely.

Combine the fruit in a large bowl; add syrup and stir to coat. Cover and chill for at least 2 hours, stirring occasionally. Drain before serving. **Yield:** 12-14 servings.

spectacular overnight slaw

Ruth Lovett, Bay City, Texas

To come up with this dish, I used a number of different recipes plus some ideas of my own. It's great for potlucks because it's made the night before and the flavor keeps getting better. Whenever I serve it, I'm inundated with recipe requests.

- 1 medium head cabbage (2-1/2 pounds), shredded
- 1 medium red onion, thinly sliced
- 1/2 cup chopped green pepper
- 1/2 cup chopped sweet red pepper
- 1/2 cup sliced stuffed olives
- 1/2 cup white wine vinegar
- 1/2 cup vegetable oil
- 1/2 cup sugar
- 2 teaspoons Dijon mustard
- 1 teaspoon *each* salt, celery seed and mustard seed

In a 4-qt. bowl, combine the cabbage, onion, peppers and olives.

In a saucepan, combine remaining ingredients; bring to a boil. Cook and stir for 1 minute. Pour over vegetables and stir gently. Cover and refrigerate overnight. Mix well before serving. **Yield:** 12-16 servings.

layered chicken salad

Joanne Trentadue, Racine, Wisconsin

I prepare this satisfying salad Saturday evening and serve it to my husband and sons on Sunday after a round of golf. It's a winner on warm days—with a unique mix of vegetables like bean sprouts, green onions, water chestnuts and pea pods. It's lovely in a glass bowl.

- 4 to 5 cups shredded iceberg lettuce
- 1 medium cucumber, thinly sliced
- 1 cup fresh bean sprouts
- 1 can (8 ounces) sliced water chestnuts, drained
- 1/2 cup thinly sliced green onions
- 1 pound fresh pea pods, halved
- 4 cups cubed cooked chicken
- 2 cups mayonnaise
- 1 tablespoon sugar
- 2 teaspoons curry powder
- 1/2 teaspoon ground ginger

Cherry tomatoes and fresh parsley sprigs, optional

Place lettuce in the bottom of a 4-qt. glass salad bowl. Layer with cucumber, bean sprouts, water chestnuts, onions, pea pods and chicken.

In a small bowl, combine mayonnaise, sugar, curry and ginger. Spread over top of salad. Garnish with cherry tomatoes and parsley if desired. Cover and chill several hours or overnight. **Yield:** 8-10 servings.

cajun potato salad

Margaret Scott, Murfreesboro, Tennessee

I have been making this mouth-watering potato salad for about 20 years. My family likes spicy foods, and thanks to a son living in New Orleans, we have a constant supply of Cajun sausage for this recipe. Made with extra sausage, it's a filling one-dish meal.

- 2 pounds small red potatoes
- 1/2 cup chopped red onion
- 1/2 cup sliced green onions
- 1/4 cup minced fresh parsley
- 6 tablespoons cider vinegar, *divided*
- 1/2 pound fully cooked kielbasa *or* Cajun sausage, sliced
- 6 tablespoons olive oil
- 1 tablespoon Dijon mustard
- 2 garlic cloves, minced
- 1/2 teaspoon pepper
- 1/4 to 1/2 teaspoon cayenne pepper

Cook the potatoes in boiling salted water for 20-30 minutes or until tender; drain. Rinse with cold water; cool completely. Cut into 1/4-in. slices; place in a large bowl. Add onions, parsley and 3 tablespoons vinegar; toss.

In a medium skillet, cook sausage in oil for 5-10 minutes or until it begins to brown. Remove with slotted spoon and add to potato mixture.

To drippings in skillet, add mustard, garlic, pepper, cayenne pepper and remaining vinegar; bring to a boil, whisking constantly. Pour over salad; toss gently. Serve immediately. **Yield:** 6 servings.

---

prize winning tips

✻Wash and dry salad greens the day before serving. I don't have a salad spinner, so I use this simple method instead: Shake excess water off greens and put them in a clean plastic bag with a sheet or two of paper toweling. Close the bag and whirl it around like a big windmill. This works just great!

Barbara McCalley, Allison Park, Pennsylvania

✻For crunchy coleslaw, cut a cabbage in half and soak it in salted water for 1 hour. Drain and proceed with the recipe.

Cheryl Maczko, Arthurdale, West Virginia

✻I add a handful of fresh cilantro with the lettuce and spinach when I make tossed salad. Cilantro's bold taste stands out against the milder greens.

Beth Walker, Round Rock, Texas

spiced peach salad

Karen Hamilton, Ludington, Michigan
This refreshing salad is my most requested recipe.
A touch of cinnamon makes it taste like fresh peach pie.
My father-in-law is an especially big fan of this fruity
salad, and I know you'll love it, too.

- 1/2 cup sugar
- 3 tablespoons vinegar
- 2 cups water
- 1 tablespoon whole cloves
- 4 cinnamon sticks
- 1 package (6 ounces) peach gelatin
- 1 can (29 ounces) peach halves

In a medium saucepan, combine sugar, vinegar and water. Tie cloves and cinnamon in a cheesecloth bag; place in the saucepan. Bring to a boil. Reduce heat; simmer, uncovered, for 10 minutes. Remove from the heat and discard spice bag. Add gelatin; stir until dissolved.

Drain peaches, reserving syrup; set peaches aside. Add water to syrup to equal 2 cups. Add to gelatin mixture; stir well. Chill until slightly thickened. Thinly slice peaches; add to gelatin. Pour into a 2-qt. glass bowl; chill until firm. **Yield:** 8-10 servings.

Editor's Note: If desired, 1/2 teaspoon ground cinnamon and 1/4 teaspoon ground cloves may be substituted for the whole spices; combine with the gelatin before adding to sugar mixture.

fruited wild rice salad

Larren Wood, Nevis, Minnesota
I created this salad recipe to feature wild rice, a delicious
state crop, plus other harvest ingredients like apples and
pecans. I make bushels of it each August when the small
nearby village of Dorset hosts several thousand visitors
at the Taste of Dorset festival.

DRESSING:
- 1/4 cup olive oil
- 1/3 cup orange juice
- 2 tablespoons honey

SALAD:
- 1 cup uncooked wild rice
- 2 Golden Delicious apples, chopped

Juice of 1 lemon
- 1 cup golden raisins
- 1 cup seedless red grapes, halved
- 2 tablespoons *each* minced fresh mint, parsley and chives

Salt and pepper to taste
- 1 cup pecan halves

Combine dressing ingredients; set aside. Cook rice according to package directions; drain if needed and allow to cool.

In a large bowl, toss the apples with lemon juice. Add raisins, grapes, mint, parsley, chives and rice. Add dressing and toss. Season with salt and pepper.

Cover and chill salad several hours or overnight. Just before serving, add the pecans and toss lightly. **Yield:** 8-10 servings.

southwestern bean salad

Lila Jean Allen, Portland, Oregon
My daughter gave me the recipe for this hearty, zippy salad. I've used it many times since and have received compliments on it. When it comes to bean salad, most people think of the sweet three-bean variety, so this slightly zesty version is a nice surprise.

- 1 can (15-1/2 ounces) kidney beans, rinsed and drained
- 1 can (15 ounces) black beans, rinsed and drained
- 1 can (15-1/2 ounces) garbanzo beans, rinsed and drained
- 2 celery ribs, sliced
- 1 medium red onion, diced
- 1 medium tomato, diced
- 1 cup frozen corn, thawed

DRESSING:
- 3/4 cup thick and chunky salsa
- 1/4 cup vegetable oil
- 1/4 cup lime juice
- 1-1/2 teaspoons chili powder
- 1 teaspoon salt
- 1/2 teaspoon ground cumin

In a bowl, combine the beans, celery, onion, tomato and corn. In a small bowl, combine all of the dressing ingredients; mix well. Pour over the bean mixture and toss to coat. Cover and chill for at least 2 hours. **Yield:** 10 servings.

parmesan vegetable toss

Judy Barbato, North Easton, Massachusetts
The first time I made this salad it was with two others for a Fourth of July party years ago. This one disappeared long before the other two! It's great for feeding a hungry crowd. At our house, there's never any left over. I hope you enjoy it as much as we do.

- 2 cups mayonnaise
- 1/2 cup grated Parmesan cheese
- 1/4 cup sugar
- 1/2 teaspoon dried basil
- 1/2 teaspoon salt
- 4 cups fresh broccoli florets (about 3/4 pound)
- 4 cups fresh cauliflowerets (about 3/4 pound)
- 1 medium red onion, sliced
- 1 can (8 ounces) sliced water chestnuts, drained
- 1 large head iceberg lettuce, torn
- 1 pound sliced bacon, cooked and crumbled
- 2 cups croutons, optional

In a large bowl, combine mayonnaise, Parmesan cheese, sugar, basil and salt. Add broccoli, cauliflower, onion and water chestnuts; toss. Cover and refrigerate for several hours or overnight.

Just before serving, place lettuce in a salad bowl and top with vegetable mixture. Sprinkle with bacon. Top with croutons if desired. **Yield:** 16-18 servings.

PEAR PLEASURE

#1

PEAR CUSTARD BARS

pear custard bars

Subtle sweetness and delightful juiciness make pears perfect for snacking and cooking. With a little imagination, creative cooks have found ways to include pears in recipes ranging from entrees to desserts.

That's the case with our Pear Pleasure contest. Cooks from coast to coast submitted over 1,800 recipes that put pears in breakfast dishes, salads and sandwiches, paired them with a variety of meats and featured them in breads, pies and pastries.

> "When I take this crowd-pleasing treat to a potluck, I come home with an empty pan..."

Jeannette Nord's change-of-pace Pear Custard Bars were our judges' top pick for the Grand Prize.

Says Jeannette from her home in San Juan Capistrano, California, "When I take this crowd-pleasing treat to a potluck, I come home with an empty pan every time. Cooking and baking come naturally to me—as a farm girl, I helped my mother feed my 10 siblings."

1/2 **cup butter, softened**
1/3 **cup sugar**
3/4 **cup all-purpose flour**
1/4 **teaspoon vanilla extract**
2/3 **cup chopped macadamia nuts**
FILLING/TOPPING:
1 **package (8 ounces) cream cheese, softened**
1/2 **cup sugar**
1 **egg**
1/2 **teaspoon vanilla extract**
1 **can (15-1/4 ounces) pear halves, drained**
1/2 **teaspoon sugar**
1/2 **teaspoon ground cinnamon**

In a mixing bowl, cream butter and sugar. Beat in the flour and vanilla until combined. Stir in the nuts. Press into a greased 8-in. square baking pan. Bake at 350° for 20 minutes or until lightly browned. Cool on a wire rack.

Increase heat to 375°. In a mixing bowl, beat cream cheese until smooth. Add sugar, egg and vanilla; mix until combined. Pour over crust. Cut pears into 1/8-in. slices; arrange in a single layer over filling. Combine sugar and cinnamon; sprinkle over pears.

Bake at 375° for 28-30 minutes (center will be soft set and will become firmer upon cooling). Cool on a wire rack for 45 minutes. Cover and refrigerate for at least 2 hours before cutting. Store in the refrigerator. **Yield:** 16 bars.

pork and pear stir-fry

Betty Phillips, French Creek, West Virginia
I've served this full-flavored stir-fry for years, always to rave reviews. Tender pork and ripe pears make a sweet combination, and a spicy sauce adds zip.

- 1/2 cup plum preserves
- 3 tablespoons soy sauce
- 2 tablespoons lemon juice
- 1 tablespoon prepared horseradish
- 2 teaspoons cornstarch
- 1/4 teaspoon crushed red pepper flakes
- 1 medium sweet yellow *or* green pepper, julienned
- 1/2 to 1 teaspoon minced fresh gingerroot
- 1 tablespoon vegetable oil
- 3 medium ripe pears, peeled and sliced
- 1 pound pork tenderloin, cut into 1/4-inch strips
- 1 can (8 ounces) sliced water chestnuts, drained
- 1-1/2 cups fresh *or* frozen snow peas
- 1 tablespoon sliced almonds, toasted

Hot cooked rice

In a bowl, combine the first six ingredients; set aside. In a skillet or wok, stir-fry yellow pepper and ginger in oil for 2 minutes. Add pears; stir-fry for 1 minute or until pepper is crisp-tender. Remove and keep warm. Stir-fry half of the pork at a time for 1-2 minutes or until meat is no longer pink.

Return pear mixture and all of the pork to pan. Add water chestnuts and reserved sauce. Bring to a boil; cook and stir for 2 minutes. Add peas; heat through. Sprinkle with almonds. Serve over rice. **Yield:** 4 servings.

pecan-pear tossed salad

Marjean Claassen, Sedgwick, Kansas
To save time, I prepare the ingredients and dressing the day before, then combine them just before serving. This salad has become a star at family gatherings. Once, when I forgot to bring it, dinner was postponed so I could go home and get it!

- 2 tablespoons fresh raspberries
- 3/4 cup olive oil
- 3 tablespoons cider vinegar
- 2 tablespoons plus 1 teaspoon sugar
- 1/4 to 1/2 teaspoon pepper

SALAD:
- 4 medium ripe pears, thinly sliced
- 2 teaspoons lemon juice
- 8 cups torn salad greens
- 2/3 cup pecan halves, toasted
- 1/2 cup fresh raspberries
- 1/3 cup (2 ounces) crumbled feta cheese

Press the raspberries through a sieve, reserving the juice. Discard the seeds. In a jar with a tight-fitting lid, combine the oil, vinegar, sugar, pepper and reserved raspberry juice; shake well. Toss the pear slices with lemon juice; drain.

In a salad bowl, combine the salad greens, pears, pecans and raspberries. Sprinkle with cheese. Drizzle with dressing. **Yield:** 8 servings.

cinnamon-swirl pear bread

Joan Anderson, Winnipeg, Manitoba
Pears add moisture to this delightful bread. Try slices toasted to go along with Sunday brunch.

>   3 cups chopped peeled ripe pears (about 3 medium)
>   1/2 cup water
> 1-1/4 cups plus 1 teaspoon sugar, *divided*
>   3 packages (1/4 ounce *each*) active dry yeast
>   1/2 cup warm water (110° to 115°)
>   4 eggs, lightly beaten
>   1/2 cup butter, softened
>   1/2 cup honey
>   2 teaspoons salt
>   1 teaspoon almond extract
>   10 to 11 cups all-purpose flour
>   1 tablespoon ground cinnamon

In a saucepan, combine pears, water and 1/2 cup sugar. Simmer, uncovered, for 10-12 minutes or until tender. Drain well, reserving syrup. Add cold water if necessary to syrup to measure 1 cup; set aside.

In a mixing bowl, dissolve yeast in warm water. Add 1 teaspoon sugar; let stand for 10 minutes. Add eggs, butter, honey, salt, extract, 4 cups flour and reserved pears and syrup. Beat until smooth. Add enough remaining flour to form a soft dough.

Turn onto a floured surface; knead until smooth and elastic, about 6-8 minutes. Place in a greased bowl, turning once to grease top. Cover and let rise in a warm place until doubled, about 1-1/4 hours.

Punch dough down; divide into thirds. Roll each portion into a 16-in. x 8-in. rectangle. Combine cinnamon and remaining 3/4 cup sugar; sprinkle over dough to within 1/2 in. of edges. Roll up jelly-roll style, starting with a short side; pinch seams to seal. Place, seam side down, in three greased 9-in. x 5-in. x 3-in. loaf pans. Cover and let rise until doubled, about 45 minutes.

Bake at 375° for 20 minutes. Cover loosely with foil. Bake 15-20 minutes longer or until bread tests done. Remove from pans to wire racks to cool. **Yield:** 3 loaves.

pear waldorf pitas

Roxann Parker, Dover, Delaware
Here's a guaranteed table-brightener for a shower, luncheon or party. Just stand back and watch these sandwiches vanish. For an eye-catching presentation, I tuck each one into a colorful folded napkin.

>   2 medium ripe pears, diced
> 1/2 cup thinly sliced celery
> 1/2 cup halved seedless red grapes
>   2 tablespoons finely chopped walnuts
>   2 tablespoons lemon yogurt
>   2 tablespoons mayonnaise
> 1/8 teaspoon poppy seeds
>   10 miniature pita pockets, halved
> Lettuce leaves

In a bowl, combine pears, celery, grapes and walnuts. In another bowl, combine yogurt, mayonnaise and poppy seeds; mix well. Add to pear mixture; toss to coat. Refrigerate for 1 hour or overnight.

To serve, line pita halves with lettuce and add 2 tablespoons pear mixture. **Yield:** 10 servings.

pear-stuffed tenderloin

Aloma Hawkins, Bixby, Missouri
*This succulent entree is a classic you'll be proud to serve
your family. There's very little fuss to making this main
dish, and the meat always turns out extremely tender.*

- 1 cup chopped peeled ripe pears
- 1/4 cup chopped hazelnuts *or* almonds, toasted
- 1/4 cup soft bread crumbs
- 1/4 cup finely shredded carrot
- 2 tablespoons chopped onion
- 1/2 teaspoon minced fresh gingerroot
- 1/4 teaspoon salt
- 1/4 teaspoon pepper
- 1 pork tenderloin (3/4 to 1 pound)

Vegetable oil
- 2 tablespoons orange marmalade

In a bowl, combine the first eight ingredients; set aside.
Make a lengthwise cut three-quarters of the way through
the tenderloin; open and flatten to 1/4-in. thickness.
Spread pear mixture over tenderloin. Roll up from a long
side; tuck in ends. Secure with toothpicks.

Place tenderloin on a rack in a shallow roasting pan.
Brush lightly with oil. Bake, uncovered, at 425° for
20-25 minutes or until a meat thermometer inserted into
pork reads 155°.

Brush with marmalade. Bake for 5-10 minutes longer
or until thermometer reads 160°-170°. Let stand for
5 minutes. Discard the toothpicks and slice. **Yield:** 2-3
servings.

pear sundae french toast

Carol Schumacher, Menoken, North Dakota
*Coming upon this creation in a potluck line, I left
with a full plate and the recipe. Now my family
oohs and aahs as soon as I bring out this
fruit-topped favorite. It's great for brunch or as
a fanciful finish to a meal.*

- 1/4 cup plus 3 tablespoons packed brown sugar,
  divided
- 6 tablespoons butter, *divided*
- 1-1/4 teaspoons ground cinnamon, *divided*
- 3 medium ripe pears, peeled and sliced
  (about 2-1/2 cups)
- 3 eggs, lightly beaten
- 3/4 cup milk
- 1 teaspoon vanilla extract
- 1/4 teaspoon ground nutmeg
- 6 slices French bread (1 inch thick)

Ice cream

In a skillet, combine 1/4 cup brown sugar, 2 tablespoons
butter and 1/4 teaspoon cinnamon; cook and stir until
sugar is dissolved. Add pears; cook until tender.

In a bowl, combine the eggs, milk, vanilla, nutmeg, and
remaining brown sugar and cinnamon. Dip bread in egg
mixture to coat each side. Melt remaining butter in a
skillet. Fry bread over medium heat for 2 minutes on
each side or until golden brown. Top with ice cream and
pear mixture. **Yield:** 6 servings.

poached pear surprise

Barbara Smith, Cannon Falls, Minnesota

Pears are my husband's favorite fruit, so he immediately declared this dessert "a keeper." It's elegant but easy, satisfying yet light. Plus, it's fun to watch the looks on the faces of our grandkids and great-grandkids when they discover the surprise filling inside.

- 4 medium ripe pears
- 1 cup water
- 1/2 cup sugar
- 1 teaspoon vanilla extract
- 1/3 cup finely chopped walnuts
- 2 tablespoons confectioners' sugar
- 1 teaspoon milk

CHOCOLATE SAUCE:
- 1/3 cup water
- 1/3 cup sugar
- 1/4 cup butter
- 1-1/3 cups semisweet chocolate chips

Fresh mint, optional

Core pears from bottom, leaving stems intact. Peel pears. Cut 1/4 in. from bottom to level if necessary. In a saucepan, bring water and sugar to a boil. Add pears; reduce heat. Cover and simmer for 10-15 minutes or until tender. Remove from the heat; stir vanilla into sugar syrup. Spoon over pears. Cover and refrigerate until chilled.

Meanwhile, combine walnuts, confectioners' sugar and milk; set aside. For chocolate sauce, combine water, sugar and butter in a small saucepan; bring to a boil. Remove from the heat; stir in chocolate chips until melted.

To serve, drain pears well; spoon nut mixture into cavities. Place on dessert plates; top with some of the chocolate sauce. Insert a mint leaf near stem if desired. Serve with the remaining chocolate sauce. **Yield:** 4 servings.

prize winning tips

✳ I ripen pears at room temperature by placing them in a paper bag with an apple. I pierce the bag in several places with the tip of a knife. Unlike most fruit, pears are ripe when they're still fairly firm.

Becky Hague, South Jordan, Utah

✳ If you're eating a pear out of hand, there's no need to peel it. Just wash it thoroughly and enjoy! The skin should always be removed, though, for cooked dishes because it will darken and toughen when heated. Use a vegetable peeler or paring knife to remove it.

Tina Corrao, Waterford, Wisconsin

✳ When peaches are out of season, I substitute pears in my favorite cobbler recipe. If your cobbler lasts more than a day, try reheating a piece in the microwave. It'll taste like it's just warm from the oven!

Betty Brown, Paisley, Ontario

runners-up

chicken in pear sauce

Andrea Lunsford, Spokane, Washington

Pairing poultry with pears brought applause from my husband and four growing children. Simple enough for everyday meals and ideal for company, this dish is a year-round standout.

    4 boneless skinless chicken breast halves
  1/2 teaspoon salt
  1/8 teaspoon white pepper
    2 tablespoons vegetable oil
    5 thick-cut bacon strips, diced
    1 can (14-1/2 ounces) chicken broth
    2 to 3 medium ripe pears, peeled and diced
    2 tablespoons cornstarch
    2 tablespoons cold water
  1/4 cup snipped chives

Sprinkle chicken with salt and pepper. In a skillet over medium heat, cook chicken in oil on both sides for about 10 minutes or until juices run clear.

Meanwhile, in a saucepan, cook bacon until crisp. Drain, reserving 1 tablespoon drippings; set bacon aside. Gradually stir broth into the drippings, scraping pan to loosen browned bits. Bring to a boil. Boil, uncovered, for 5 minutes.

Add pears; return to a boil. Boil, uncovered, for 5 minutes or until pears are tender. Combine cornstarch and water until smooth; add the chives. Gradually stir into pear sauce; bring to a boil. Cook and stir for 2 minutes or until thickened and bubbly. Stir in bacon. Serve over the chicken. **Yield:** 4 servings.

blue cheese pear salad

Sherry Duval, Baltimore, Maryland

Guests at a barbecue we hosted one summer brought this cool, refreshing salad. Now it's a mainstay at most all our cookouts. The mingling of zesty tastes and textures instantly wakes up the taste buds.

   10 cups torn salad greens
    3 large ripe pears, peeled and cut into large pieces
  1/2 cup thinly sliced green onions
    4 ounces crumbled blue cheese
  1/4 cup slivered almonds, toasted
MUSTARD VINAIGRETTE:
  1/3 cup olive oil
    3 tablespoons red wine vinegar
1-1/2 teaspoons sugar
1-1/2 teaspoons Dijon mustard
    1 garlic clove, minced
  1/2 teaspoon salt
Pepper to taste

In a large bowl, combine the salad greens, pears, onions, cheese and almonds. In a jar with a tight-fitting lid, combine the vinaigrette ingredients; shake well. Pour over salad; toss to coat. Serve immediately. **Yield:** 8-10 servings.

caramel pear pie

Mary Kaehler, Lodi, California
A dear friend shared the recipe for this attractive pie. The caramel drizzle and streusel topping make it almost too pretty to eat. Knowing this dessert is waiting is great motivation for our children to eat all their vegetables.

- 6 **cups sliced peeled ripe pears (about 6 medium)**
- 1 **tablespoon lemon juice**
- 1/2 **cup plus 3 tablespoons sugar, *divided***
- 2 **tablespoons quick-cooking tapioca**
- 3/4 **teaspoon ground cinnamon**
- 1/4 **teaspoon salt**
- 1/4 **teaspoon ground nutmeg**
- 1 **unbaked pastry shell (9 inches)**
- 3/4 **cup old-fashioned oats**
- 1 **tablespoon all-purpose flour**
- 1/4 **cup cold butter**
- 18 **caramels**
- 5 **tablespoons milk**
- 1/4 **cup chopped pecans**

In a large bowl, combine pears and lemon juice. In another bowl, combine 1/2 cup sugar, tapioca, cinnamon, salt and nutmeg. Add to pears; stir gently. Let stand for 15 minutes. Pour into pastry shell. In a bowl, combine oats, flour and remaining sugar. Cut in butter until crumbly. Sprinkle over pears. Bake at 400° for 45 minutes.

Meanwhile, in a saucepan over low heat, melt caramels with milk. Stir until smooth; add pecans. Drizzle over pie. Bake 8-10 minutes longer or until crust is golden brown and filling is bubbly. Cool on a wire rack. **Yield:** 6-8 servings.

almond pear tartlets

Marie Rizzio, Traverse City, Michigan
Although they're quick to fix, you'll want to savor these pretty pastries slowly. Delicately spiced pears are complemented by an almond sauce and a crispy crust. Be prepared to share the recipe.

- 1 **egg, lightly beaten**
- 1/2 **cup plus 6 tablespoons sugar, *divided***
- 3/4 **cup heavy whipping cream**
- 2 **tablespoons butter, melted**
- 1/2 **teaspoon almond extract**
- 1 **package (10 ounces) frozen puff pastry shells, thawed**
- 2 **small ripe pears, peeled and thinly sliced**
- 1/2 **teaspoon ground cinnamon**
- 1/8 **teaspoon ground ginger**
- 1/2 **cup slivered almonds, toasted, optional**

In a saucepan, combine the egg, 1/2 cup sugar, cream and butter. Cook and stir until the sauce is thickened and a thermometer reads 160°. Remove from the heat; stir in extract. Cover and refrigerate.

On an unfloured surface, roll each pastry into a 4-in. circle. Place in an ungreased 15-in. x 10-in. x 1-in. baking pan. Top each with pear slices. Combine cinnamon, ginger and remaining sugar; sprinkle over the pears.

Bake at 400° for 20 minutes or until the pastry is golden brown. Sprinkle with almonds if desired. Serve warm with the chilled cream sauce. **Yield:** 6 servings.

general recipe index